Books by Catherine Drinker Bowen

FRIENDS AND FIDDLERS

BELOVED FRIEND
The Story of Tchaikowsky and Nadejda von Meck
  (In Collaboration with B. von Meck)

FREE ARTIST
The Story of Anton and Nicholas Rubenstein

YANKEE FROM OLYMPUS
Justice Holmes and His Family

JOHN ADAMS AND THE
  AMERICAN REVOLUTION

THE WRITING OF BIOGRAPHY

THE LION AND THE THRONE
The Life and Times of Sir Edward Coke

Adventures of a Biographer

Adventures of a Biographer

By Catherine Drinker Bowen

An Atlantic Monthly Press Book

Little, Brown and Company
BOSTON • TORONTO

ATLANTIC-LITTLE, BROWN BOOKS
ARE PUBLISHED BY
LITTLE, BROWN AND COMPANY
IN ASSOCIATION WITH
THE ATLANTIC MONTHLY PRESS

Published simultaneously in Canada
by Little, Brown & Company (Canada) Limited

PRINTED IN THE UNITED STATES OF AMERICA

For my brother, Henry S. Drinker

Preface

In this book I have described the biographer's way of life, which to my mind is a pleasant way; I hope I may pursue it for some years to come. My chapters have no thesis and no particular aim, informational or otherwise; this is not a treatise for writers. The preparation of a long biography is an outdoor as well as an indoor exercise; my books have led me on many journeys. I have not tried to take the reader step by step along the way, or stressed the preliminary digging and real day labor that goes into the compilation of a history. Rather, I have told about the people and places I have met on my research travels, from Philadelphia to California, to Leningrad, Berlin or Boston, Massachusetts, as the case might be . . . Intourist guides, English earls, college professors of history, Beacon Hill ladies, courthouse janitors, lawyers, librarians, judges on the bench . . . challengers, friends, helpers, and the stranger who set me on my way.

For the most part there has been, for me, pleasure in the recollection. And where there was pain, I have set it down with the rest. In his Autobiography, *Edward Gibbon says that he has "always condemned the practice of transforming a private memorial into a vehicle of satire or praise." A noble sentiment, worthy of the author of* The Decline and Fall of the Roman Empire. *Yet I for one cannot measure up to it, nor do I think I really believe in measuring up to it. The past without pain does not exist and if it did, it would make dull reading. Every book that I have written has had its situations and its people who rose up to block me, either purposefully or by accident. This is the biographer's hazard, and when it happens the writer fights back, no holds barred either in the doing or the telling.*

I have not always kept to strict chronology in these reminiscences. At times I have used real names and at times, disguised ones; I trust that no offense will be taken where, indeed, none was meant. Writing biography is exciting business. Like courtship, it has its moments of gratification and its days of despair, when history closes her doors and will not show her face. Every writer lives a double life — the life of reality and the life of illusion; the biographer who wishes to make his characters believed in, must let his imagination run. To re-create the past is no less a task, artistically, than to write a novel or an epic poem; material must be looked for in life as well as in old books and records. The historian, it has been said, must know how men live who are not historians; he must have an interest in his neighbors, else how can he recognize, in history, "affinities in strange disguises"?

For an author there is embarrassment in the presentation of personal reminiscence. Why should one suppose that an incident is interesting, merely because it happened to oneself? Twenty years ago, I published a book of personal essays, called Friends and Fiddlers — *about myself, it is true, yet primarily about chamber music and the pleasures of playing with one's friends. This second book of reminiscence, by that same token, has more of history and scholarship, I trust, than of me. For forty years I have been writing biography; if I had to choose, I would live the biographer's life over again. I cannot conceive of time spent more entertainingly, to myself if to no one else.*

I wish to thank the Atlantic Monthly *for permission to reprint "John Adams' Bowl" and "Salute to Librarians";* Harper's Magazine *for permission to use some paragraphs from "The Magnificence of Age." None of the other pieces has been published, though here and there I have quoted or paraphrased a line from my own biographies.*

Contents

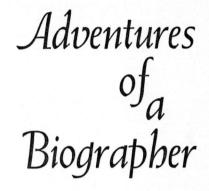

Adventures
of
a
Biographer

The Present and the Past: Moscow

"Do not go to Russia," said Barbara von Meck. The biography of Tchaikovsky was finished; we had been collaborators, our book was in print and I had begun work on a biography of Tchaikovsky's teachers, the brothers Anton and Nicholas Rubinstein. Madame von Meck, a White Russian, had fled her country in 1917 at the outbreak of revolution.

She looked at me seriously as she spoke. "The country has changed, the people are no longer as I knew them and as you have learned to know them. Rich and poor are dressed alike on the streets, they tell me. In Moscow the churches are defaced, the bells are gone, the watchdogs at the porters' gates are gone. I don't know what you will see, but it will not be the Mother Russia that Tchaikovsky knew, and the Rubinsteins knew."

She shook her head. "You will lose your vision," she said.

It was eleven at night when my train approached the Polish border. I had come from Berlin; this was 1937 and there was no question of flying. New York was still a solid two weeks' journey from Moscow. The Russian ambassador, Troyanovsky, had given me a visa after some persuasion, and I had letters to the Commissar for Education, the Director of the Moscow Conservatory and others. I had chosen to ignore Barbara von Meck's warning. Having written one book about Russia without ever seeing the country, I was not going to hazard a second such performance. Russians who had read *Beloved Friend* wrote to say that my intimate descriptions of Moscow made them homesick; I must have lived many years in their country to know it so well? This, no doubt, was what Madame von Meck had meant by my "vision." Actually, a large part of this descriptive detail had come out of old nineteenth-century Russian guidebooks — homely items such as the nighttime tap of the watchman's stick on Moscow's wooden footways, the noisy whir of his rattle. (Guidebooks warned travelers against this sound, advising them to engage rooms at the rear of the house.)

To me the final effect of these garnered details savored more of luck than of vision, as if I had written my book by incantation. Moreover, the years of reading had made me extremely curious about Russia; I needed to see if my descriptions were valid. No country in history had changed its face so rapidly and so radically. Imperial Russia was indeed gone. The places where Anton Rubinstein had played piano to the Tsarina, the Salle de la Noblesse in Petersburg, the English Club in Moscow where all night Nicholas Rubinstein risked his money at écarté — these had suffered a sea-change, metamorphosed by the Comrades into railway brotherhood clubs, anti-religious museums or palaces of culture for the proletariat.

But the Moscow Conservatory still stood and was in use,

brilliantly in use if all I heard were true, and the same with Anton Rubinstein's Conservatory in St. Petersburg . . . I must learn to call it Leningrad, von Meck had said grimly. Oh well, I had replied, if I learned nothing else in Russia, I would discover which trees put out their spring leaves first along the Nevsky Prospekt — a matter we had debated futilely. "The Bolsheviks haven't changed the *climate*," I argued. Madame von Meck, shaking her head, had said she was not so sure.

And now I was on my way — that selfsame way taken a hundred years ago by young Anton Rubinstein, returning from his years of education and concert playing on the Continent. As a boy of ten, a *Wunderkind,* he had gone out from Russia with his teacher, François Villoing, traveling by diligence, and he had returned in the year 1848, when Europe was stirring with revolution. Now I traveled the same long road eastward, across the Great North German Plain. It was early April, the fields were drowned in water from a winter's snow, the roads no more than wheel ruts, frozen deep. Before the dark closed down I saw above the brooks the willows toss their dry brown streamers in a wind that reached, I knew, clear down from Finland.

With my nose against the windowpane I watched the border station lights approach, felt the big train brake to a stop. My only companion in the compartment was a fat Polish-American woman from Chicago, on her way to visit relatives in Warsaw. Very nervous about traveling, she had sat all the way with her feet up, resting them on a pink knitted shawl as if the floor might hold contamination. Repeatedly she had told me "not to trust nobody on this train only our two selves." My own breast being warm with expectation and general excitement, this only made me laugh, which seemed to throw my companion into utmost gloom and foreboding.

Passport kontrol! Somewhere down the train the words were barked. It came to my mind that Anton Rubinstein had had a terrible time passing through Poland in the year 1848. At the border, Russian officials had confiscated his trunkful of musical manuscript, all his youthful compositions for five years back. "Notes?" they said angrily. "What kind of *notes* are these? Anarchists and revolutionists write in cipher that looks just like musical notation. We must seal up this trunk until it can be investigated."

All this had happened long ago, I told myself, and in a revolutionary year. Today was 1937 and my papers were in perfect order. . . .

There was a tramp of footsteps in the corridor. At our compartment door appeared four Polish policemen, costumed stylishly in blue and red, each with a lantern hung on his chest containing a lighted candle. I had time only to notice that all four were young and handsome, when their chief sang out the word *"Green-kair!"* on a rising inflection, as if he were calling a station stop.

He must have repeated it three times before I realized that he was talking to me. *Drinker!* Of course. Catherine Drinker-Bowen; in Europe for some reason I am always hyphenated. What the young policeman made of the three words was charming and bore little relation to my name as I had known it. I smiled and stepped forward, passport in hand. The chief smiled back at me, behind him his three henchmen waited. Flipping over the leaves of my passport, the chief frowned and turned to his friends. A confabulation ensued in Polish, accompanied by shruggings of the shoulders and shakings of the head, after which the chief informed me in German that I had no Polish visa. A Russian visa, yes. A visa for France and for Germany. But not for Poland. And one must traverse Poland to reach Russia, yes?

Politely but vigorously I told him that of course I had a Polish visa. In New York my literary agent had tended to everything. A most reliable gentleman, who never made mistakes. Would the Herr Kapitan be pleased to glance again? He would surely find it. "Look!" I said, pointing. "There it is."

No no, there it was *not*. That, Frau Greenkair-Boyen, was the visa for Russia . . . I would have to get off the train. I could remain in the station until the next train back to Berlin. Perhaps ten hours, perhaps twenty . . .

My dismay and astonishment were genuine. Maybe the officers sensed it; at any rate they paused and the chief began to question me. Why was I going to Russia? I was a writer, I said. *Schriftsteller*. (My German is scanty, I could not launch into biographical explanations.) *Schriftsteller?* They repeated. On what journal? "I am *Musikkritikerin*," I replied, evading the issue — and in truth I had once written musical articles for the press. "Ahhh!" they breathed. *"Sie ist eine Musikkritikerin."* They smiled, became pleasantly animated and my heart that had been a cold lump in my chest began once more to function. (Shades of Chopin and Wieniawski, what a lovely, musical country!) I put up a left arm, tucked my chin down and drew an imaginary bow. *"Ich bin eine Geigerin,"* I said, grinning. "I play the violin."

If I had announced myself as Titania, Queen of the Fairies, the *Polizei-beamten* could not have shown more pleasure. "Ahhh, *sie spielt Geige*." They laughed, they chattered, there was a second conference in Polish. The chief turned to me. "If you were a man," he said, "I would not do this. But seeing you are a Frau, you may come with me into the station and pay a dollar, and I will give you a pass."

We got off the train, all five of us. The chief took my arm, I looked up at him admiringly. He was indeed a prince of the blood, this *Polizei-beamte,* and my fate lay in his hands. While he conferred at the customs desk, the other three officers assured me that I did not appreciate my luck, nobody went through without a visa. Lately, in particular, since the troubles in Moscow . . . I knew at once what they meant. The first two purge trials had been in all the newspapers. And though the phrase *brainwash* was not yet invented, our world had been shocked by the forced confessions of those prisoners, their terrible abject admissions of guilt. . . .

Forms were handed to me. I filled them out and saw my passport stamped — oh blessed, thumping sound! The customs officer opened my bags. I took out my American cigarettes and distributed them, to the last Chesterfield. The chief bowed, I bowed, we shook hands, I ran for the train and boarded with a coltish leap of joy. In my compartment the Polish-American woman, long since certain she had seen the last of me, rose to her feet and crossed herself as the train moved over the border.

All next day I watched the Russian plain go by, monotonous, dry and poor. Farm horses shied as we swept past, behind a solitary bicyclist the dust rose. I had crossed our Kansas plains and the Texas prairies — but the land was not like this. In all the wide brown country the birches were the only point one's eye could rest upon. They stood in groves or solitary; in this harsh landscape their grace was like a reprieve. No wonder the Russians sang ballads about them: *"In the field there stands a birch tree . . ."* Sheep ran from us, tumbling and jostling; geese scurried off, wings lifted. Men dressed in sheepskin jackets plowed the land, felt-booted, their women walked beside them barefoot. In this eternal blow the windmills whirled. Early on that second afternoon the hills began to rise; the plowed furrows took on curves. A peasant galloped by, barebacked on a shaggy horse. His village lay far off behind a clump of poplars — log huts that must have provided miserable shelter. One felt the north even from this heated train; at dusk the April sky wore clear cold colors and on the fields, cloud shadows took on magic tints. Snow lay in sheltered places, under the bank above the railroad and in the poplar groves. For a mile, now and then, I told myself this could be New England — but there were no stones and no stone walls. No hedges even, between the fields.

In my notebook I set it all down and felt myself strangely stirred. Tchaikovsky had adored this poor country, these barren husks of fields. So had the brothers Rubinstein, though they were southern born, from Bessarabia, and Anton at least was Western in his ways. One time, returning from Italy, when the train first halted on home soil, Tchaikovsky had thrown himself flat down and kissed the ground. Even Anton Rubinstein, for all his Continental manners, shed tears when his foot touched earth. "Here she is," he said. "Mother Russia!"

Odd, how a dead man's thinking can penetrate one's skull, making one suddenly and absurdly no foreigner but a person traveling toward *home!* The train drew into Moscow station, I got off and stood looking up the platform, past the hurrying shapes of strangers. Perhaps I would fail, in this crazy pilgrimage. Perhaps von Meck had been right and I would lose my "vision." They would put obstacles in my way —so people had told me. The red tape of socialism can be a chilling, killing thing.

But whatever they did, they could not take from me this journey across the Northern Plain, and all that I had seen and felt.

"I do not know if today is Sunday," Emily said coldly. "Tomorrow is Rest Day and then we have five Work Days. I have told you before, about our Soviet calendar. Comrade Boyen, why are you so old-fashioned?"

Emily was my Intourist guide, whose services for thirty days I had bought and paid for in New York. She was twenty-three years old, small and pretty, blue-eyed, with dark hair and a white smooth skin. She wore at all times a neat woolen suit with shirt and necktie; a cigarette was never out of her mouth and she seemed born to baffle me at every turn. In New York I had specified that my guide must be musically trained. Her main function would be translating from Russian in the libraries of Moscow and Leningrad; she would be of little use to me unless she knew music.

Emily, as it developed, was a graduate of the University of Moscow. And she knew not one word of music or of history before 1905. When I asked her to translate inscriptions on tombstones or over church doors she stood silent, her lips working helplessly. "I do not know these words. These are not political words. They are perhaps Bible words? I will ask my grandmother."

What we should have done without Emily's grandmother, her *babushka,* I cannot think. Over the telephone Emily's *babushka* let me know when it was Monday and when it was Saturday; she sent scraps of paper written over in Russian which turned out to be paraphrases of lines from Isaiah or Proverbs, in words that Emily could translate into English. Eventually she even prevailed upon Emily to address me in the fine old style as Ekaterina Genrichovna — Catherine, daughter of Henry — instead of Comrade, which I found gruesome and said so. (But such pleasantries came later, when Emily had begun to laugh.) During these first weeks, Emily was dead serious and I was irritable from being balked and blocked and shoved about. "Moscow," I wrote home, "is poor, shabby, dirty and filled with spirit. The streets are crowded with young people and nobody young has any manners. In the tramcars they knock you down bodily and never even look round. In the theater the fleas bite my legs and make me jump as if I had hiccoughs."

But it was not fleas and dirt that bothered me. After all, this was a country not yet recovered from revolution; one did not look for physical comfort. What bothered me was the fact that no one would believe what I said. My statement that I had come to Russia to study the Rubinstein brothers was received with blank rude stares. Intourist had heard the names; the brothers were revered as national heroes. "But why should an American woman wish to write about the Rubinsteins?" At the hotel bureau I showed Intourist my biography of Tchaikovsky. They read the name von Meck under mine on the cover and went no further. The von Mecks were aristocrats, they said stiffly. Exiles, traitors to their country.

It was the first time in my life I had been looked on as a

calculating liar; the experience unnerved me. Intourist took my letters of introduction and kept them, putting me off each day with promises or that shrug of the shoulders I had come to know and dread. In my hotel room my suitcases were searched; the handles were removed from my balcony doors so they could not be locked. It all seemed very elaborate and a great waste of time. The precious days went by and I had not visited Nicholas Rubinstein's Moscow Conservatory, nor Tchaikovsky's house at suburban Klin, nor the Rubinstein Museum. They did not say No, or forbid me. Simply, I found myself eternally somewhere else. In despair I followed Emily on daily tour . . . to the Anti-Religious Museum, the Syphilis Clinic, the Museum of the Revolution, the Ball Bearing Factory, where machines thumped and clicked and gurgled and Emily admonished me to observe our happy Soviet workers, so many times more contented than the workers in capitalist U.S.A.

A friend of mine had lately traveled to the U.S.S.R. to see the Russian theater. She told Intourist point-blank that she would not go near a factory or a clinic. As a result she was not permitted to set foot in a theater, not once. Thus forewarned, I told Emily, morning after morning, that this was the finest anti-religious museum or syphilis clinic or Siberian-marble subway station I had ever seen in my life. (It was, too, for obvious reasons.) In the evenings when Emily left me I went to the theater or to the movies next door to my hotel, where the poster advertised a drama called *Tom Sawyer*. Here I saw the hero, "Nigger Jim," flogged cruelly, to the evident ideological triumph of three young Soviet citizens behind me who leaned forward, pointed to the scene, then pointed at me.

At the Bolshoi Theater I fared better. Sitting in a box with five good-natured soldiers and a large pock-marked Moscow policeman, I saw the play called *Pickwick Club*. Onto the stage at curtain rising rolled the coach, carrying Mr. Pickwick and the Fat Boy, sound asleep. Avgoosta Snodgrassa, Dodsona and Fogga, Mr. Pickwick climbing the wall . . . I saw them all and laughed until I cried. No English actors could have done it half so well and above all so *Englishly*. This was a people talented for the theater beyond any Western dream. I saw Tchaikovsky's operas, *Eugene Oniegin* and *Pique Dame,* magnificently staged. All this I saw and marveled at, but I was not happy. The brothers Rubinstein were farther from me than they had been ten days ago when I landed at the Moscow station. Perhaps von Meck had indeed been right and I should not have come here. "Emily," I would say hopefully, each morning when she arrived in my hotel room. "Can't you organize a tour to the Conservatory library this afternoon, so we can do some translating?"

Organizing a tour, in this case, meant the two of us walking five blocks from the Moskva Hotel to where the Conservatory sat on Hertzen Street, a yellow stucco house behind its iron fence. Every day since arrival I had walked there and stood staring, like a prisoner on the wrong side of the bars. Through discreet queries or perhaps a kind of loving, desiring osmosis, I learned which floor the library was on and where the students' concert hall was situated. The Rubinstein Museum, which I must see or perish, was in the new building, above the concert hall. One morning I did not wait for Emily but went off alone. Suddenly she appeared, where I stood looking through the iron spikes. Without a sign beyond her usual mysterious smile, she turned in, pushed open the heavy Conservatory doors and beckoned me to follow.

What had cracked the hard shell of Emily's Intourist bosses I will never know. But cracked it was and softened. Perhaps my good behavior counted, or my admiring loud tourism at factory and clinic. At any rate, from then on, doors opened. I cannot say that I was welcomed, but at least I was not shut out. Up three flights of stairs in Nicholas Rubinstein's famous, ever to be honored Conservatory walked Emily with me behind her, seeking the library, then seeking the card catalogue, the books, a place to sit. After we had repeated this on six successive mornings, the felt-slippered lady librarians began to favor us with cold nods of recognition; even the peasant woman at the library door gave us our pink admittance slips without the usual argument. We left our coats and hats outside in the hallway. "Because of disease," said Emily.

We sat at a battered long table translating — in whispers — old Russian musical newspapers. Every seat at the table was occupied by students — girls, boys, old men and women, copying music or studying. They were the shabbiest, most uncombed persons I had ever seen within four walls. They were also the most eager at their work, and my heart went out to them.

But if theirs went out to me, they did not show it. Sometimes they would smile at me, but, their eyes lighting on Emily's Intourist badge, they would look quickly down. Accredited persons had told me Intourist was first cousin to the secret police, but I was slow to believe it. On the wall behind us hung a large, framed photograph of Nicholas Rubinstein, in dress clothes, his mustachios drooping. This was indeed his Conservatory; he had founded it, built it with monies garnered from the nobility. He had directed it and taught Western music to Moscow — Beethoven, Mendelssohn, Bach. And the city had responded with adoration. This was a man of irresistible charm, whether he sat at the piano or made merry with his friends.

Nicholas's eyes were sad in the picture. Looking down over his low collar and string tie he seemed tired and ill, sophisticated, sensitive and very much the artist. There is a peculiar cast to the musical face everywhere; even in repose one sees the promise of mobility and quick response. This photograph must have been taken late in life, I thought, just before the fatal trip to Paris. How characteristic of Nicholas Gregorovitch, to call from his Parisian bed for a dozen cold oysters and an ice, eat them with satisfaction — and die! Directly below the photograph, so close that my chair bumped if I pushed too far back, was a bronze bust of Lenin in his worker's cap, looking anything but sophisticated — looking indeed as if he could bite off and swallow the Conservatory and me with it.

Here in Moscow I was not searching for manuscript sources. The hardest part of my work, the digging part and the historical survey, had been done at home. Nor was I looking for musical scores. These I had seen in Berlin at the *Staatsbibliothek,* which boasted ten bound volumes of Anton Rubinstein's signed scores, with his own expression marks and stage directions. I had studied his operas — *Kalashnikoff, Der Dämon, Das Verlorene Paradies,* — the *Ocean Symphony* and the ballets. And each score more appallingly tedious than the one before . . . *Die Rebe* (The Vine) rife with nymphs and fauns, with scenes at the Court of Bacchus. "*Satyrs agitent des cymbales et des tympanoux,"* the score directed. And, as the dying heroine was carried on stage, *"Consternation générale."*

Running my eye down the inked pages, my own consternation had mounted. Though I knew well that Anton Rubinstein's genius was for performance rather than for composition, I was discouraged by the profusion of banal harmonies and jagged melodic lines. "Tremolo and bang!" my notebook said. "Hold it, Suleika, on high C and let your breath out thriftily." And written very black, "God be praised I don't have to sit through this performance."

Oddly enough, the scores in no way diminished my respect for Rubinstein. Nobody in two hemispheres had played the piano so well . . . Anton Rubinstein, shaking his mane above the keys in Paris, London, Stuttgart, New York — Anton *was* the pianoforte. And how I wished that I could have heard him teach his pupils! In three words he could characterize a musical phrase. There was little mercy in Anton Gregorovitch; one morning he tapped a well-born young Englishwoman on the shoulder when she had played her piece. "Too much Belgrave Square," he said. He feared neither Tsar nor devil; he had played in palaces and starved in garrets, and his life was lived for music.

What I wanted from these Russian libraries was not musical history but biographical detail, personal gossip and anecdote, the memoirs of friends and relatives. In old magazines, pamphlets and musical gazettes I found it abundantly. The writers were frank, they revealed bits I had not dreamed of. About Serge Taneyeff, for instance — Tchaikovsky's loyal friend, a profound musical scholar whose taste, in a florid era, was classic, impeccable and severe. . . . Odd, that I had

never discovered Taneyeff's character, though in Paris, old
Monsieur Kamensky had hinted at it when he talked to me
of Tchaikovsky. But Tchaikovsky's sins were mild, I found
now, compared with these. If certain letters could be relied
on, Taneyeff was a corrupter of youth to such extent the
Conservatory came near to being wrecked by him. My notebook burst into indignant moralism. "Musicians! Try to write
their lives and you never find it exemplary. Again an idol
broken. Taneyeff the pure, the clean, the dedicated. How they
all said it! And here I find his private life a sink of abnor-
mality and sensuality. Is this why they are artists? I would
like to write about a good man."

It was an odd reaction and, under the circumstances,
hardly permissible. I could not know that I was later to act
upon it to the extent of three biographies, though the words
"good man" are suspect and their definition differs on every
tongue. Concerning the Moscow gossip, perhaps I could have
found tidbits at home, in the New York Public Library and
elsewhere. But I could never have found such rich profusion
of photographs. Here were my dramatis personae, laid out
for me to view, to gaze upon and linger over until I knew
them as friends. . . . Napravnik, with his imperial and his
gold watch chain. Serge Taneyeff. Jurgenson the music publisher, full-bearded like Brahms. Tchaikovsky, standing on
the Conservatory steps. Stasov, Rimsky-Korsakov, Ossip
Gabrilovitch as a boy, in white frilled collar and velvet suit.
Anton Rubinstein, as painted by Repin, in full dress with his
conductor's baton — blue-eyed, his mustache light brown,
handsome almost as Liszt. Nicholas Rubinstein with his hair
frisé, the mouth sensuous and full under his mustache, the
forehead high. Czar of Music, Moscow called Nicholas. Thun-

der Hurler. For love of Nicholas Rubinstein, young women committed suicide, done dramatically after the imperial Russian manner, on a concert evening at the Salle de la Noblesse, with Nicholas's photograph clasped to the lady's satin bosom. . . .

One evening, by a simple ruse of Emily's, I got upstairs to the forbidden Rubinstein Museum. To this day the incident puzzles me — was my admission by accident or design? The Moscow Conservatory was holding a series of student concerts, with participants from all over the U.S.S.R. The Director had told me point-blank that I could not attend. All the seats were taken, he said. The Museum being over the concert hall, and the hall being opened only for performance, the Museum was unattainable without a concert ticket. On this particular evening Emily and I had stayed late at the library upstairs; we came past the concert hall foyer at 7:30, just as the concert was beginning. Standing by a revolving gate was a young man who greeted Emily warmly. He was a newspaper critic, I learned later, and quite evidently a beau of Emily's. Without the slightest hesitation he took us both in on his pass. Emily followed him to the concert; I flew up three flights of stairs as if the witches were after me, found the Museum and literally flung myself into the arms of its Director, an old man who had studied piano with Nicholas Rubinstein. He welcomed me, and for two hours displayed his treasures.

When I went downstairs the concert was just over, my notebook was full and I was to the last degree exhilarated. For the ensuing week I attended the concerts every night by myself; the gatekeeper simply nodded in recognition and let me by. The students played like angels, the Red Army Chorus sang and danced with infinite vigor and enthusiasm. On the second night a little old lady sat next to me, her head tied in a peasant scarf; her hands in her black woolen lap were scarred with hard work. After the first piece had been played she nudged me and smiled shyly, gesticulating toward the stage to know if I had enjoyed the performance. "*Kharasho* — wonderful!" I said, from my meager Russian vocabulary. The old lady seemed delighted, she passed me surreptitious pieces of chocolate from a paper bag and we were friends. At intermission I roamed the old building — Nicholas Rubinstein's building — to my heart's content, hearing behind closed doors imaginary fiddles, the pianistic scales of pupils. My head was daft with scenes and faces, I began to think in terms of chapter headings and print.

Next morning, Emily told me the old lady had been her grandmother. "I wanted my *babushka* to meet you," Emily said — and she said no more. I did not ask why I had not been warned beforehand. I knew it was not safe for me to greet Emily's relative in public as a friend. She might, next day, have simply disappeared. No one said the word Siberia. "Sent east," the expression was, that year. "So-and-so has been sent east, did you know?"

Past and present, today and yesterday . . . At the Bolshoi Theater the Tsar's box was draped in Communist red, stamped with the hammer and sickle. The yellow brocade stage curtain bore revolutionary dates: 1871, 1905, 1917. But when the curtain rose we were in Tchaikovsky's Russia, the Russia I was searching for, where grand dukes walked through curtseying drawing rooms, and where at dawn Eugene Oniegin fought his pistol duel.

Next day, in morning streets around the Kremlin Square, I saw the Cossack soldiers swagger, their black astrakhan hats cocked jauntily, their long belted coats reaching almost to the ground. Handsome creatures; beside them the Russian women looked mere shapeless bundles of clothes. Waiting in line to enter Lenin's tomb, I saw great fierce-eyed men, dark-skinned, wearing peaked military caps above broad Mongol cheekbones. From Central Asia, Emily told me, glancing at them respectfully. I looked at them and felt the East. In those strange hard faces something terrified me; if I died on the spot I knew those brown hands would not stoop to lift me. There was a fatalism about death, here in this city; one recognized it constantly. At the American Embassy I had heard the story of an English girl tourist who fell into a street cavity — Moscow was pitted with gaping holes over which one passed on a single board plank. She fell and simply disappeared. A week later her friends found her in a hospital, still unconscious, recognizable only from her plaid woolen skirt.

In the afternoons when Emily left me I walked alone through the city, around the Kremlin wall and along the river where Tchaikovsky had so often walked and where one night he tried to drown himself from grief — in water that was just waist deep. On these walks I was besieged with beggars, starved miserable men and women whose rags scarcely covered them. Once I saw, standing against a closed door, a neatly dressed man, motionless and very tall, whose face was the terrible bloodless color of old parchment. I approached him, horrified, pretending not to look, and as I passed he fell full to the ground and lay there. I thought that he was dead. I turned back and stooped to touch him;

a soldier shouted at me and ran toward us, waving me angrily away. . . . Next day when I told Emily, she said these beggars were worthless persons who refused to work or to enter homes for the aged.

Russia was indeed poor, this year of 1937; the signs of poverty were everywhere. It was only four years since the famine in the Ukraine, when Stalin chose to starve three million dissident kulaks. But Russia would not admit to poverty. Everything must be perfect in this first socialist state, all evil resided in capitalist countries. I told myself I had never been so consistently proselytized. And what a talent Moscow had for dramatic presentation, outside the theater as well as in! At night the Red Square was illumined by floodlights; as the clock struck twelve one heard the Kremlin chimes give out the *Internationale*. No one, it seemed, went to bed in Moscow; at two in the morning the streets were still faintly light with yesterday. When June came, this northern summer would have no night. (Through just such early morning streets, Nicholas Rubinstein had walked on his way to cards at the English Club, coming home hours later to be greeted by his grumbling, faithful valet, Agathon.)

Today and yesterday . . . The fantastic domes and spires of St. Basil, myself climbing up with Emily until a sudden roar from the sky brought us tumbling down the steps and outside to the Red Square. The Air Fleet flew above us in beautiful formation, rehearsing for the May Day celebrations. . . . Beside Lenin's tomb a grandstand had been erected and Voroshilov, Marshal of the Army, reviewed the show, surrounded by his officers. "In the days of Nicholas I," I told Emily dreamily, "Moscow had military maneuvers, too. And grand dukes stood saluting, just like Marshal Voroshilov."

"Ekaterina Genrichovna!" Emily said. "All tourists but yourself desire to see what is new in the U.S.S.R. You alone want to see the old, you alone speak of the old as if yesterday were now. Very well! Tomorrow I will take you to the old Dog Market. There are no dogs because dogs are dirty and eat meat that cannot be spared. But I will take you there."

It was Emily's first open, expressed capitulation. My impulse was to throw my arms around her and kiss her on both cheeks. But I knew better — and I had learned my lesson hard. Whatever happened, throughout these Russian days and nights, the victory must be hers, not mine. The Comrades were not to be dented by argument. Is a Utah Mormon convinced by argued atheism, or a Seventh Day Adventist by news of Karma and of Heaven won through reincarnation? In a socialist country, humility becomes a capitalist. And I, who needed Emily's help each day, each hour, had learned perforce the semblance of humility.

There in the street I bowed to Emily, hand on my breast. "In the name of Anton Gregorovitch Rubinstein and the great Commonwealth of Pennsylvania," I said, "I salute you and thank you, Emily, *dooshenka*."

To my astonishment and gratification, Emily laughed.

2

The Present and the Past: Leningrad and Klin

Perhaps all cities keep, through the centuries, their especial character and the marks of their origin. Leningrad is only four hundred miles from Moscow. Yet it is still Peter the Great's city — or was when I went there with Emily — as different from old Moscow as New York is different from Boston. Tsar Peter built this city on the marshes by the Gulf of Finland, early in the eighteenth century. He made it his capital, laying it out with elegance after the Western fashion, in handsome squares ornamented with prancing statuary and bordered with rococo palaces, or with yellow stucco buildings, pillared classically in white, that might have been designed by Thomas Jefferson.

Actually, these classic buildings were designed by Rossi, imported from Italy for the purpose. Peter's city was planned by Rossi and by Rastrelli, who favored a kind of Russian baroque — palaces copied after Versailles, with gilded figures standing on the roof. Today the statues are gone, done in by dampness or by the Comrades. But in the public squares I met everywhere with tsars and generals, sculptured on horseback. In the old Senate Square, Tsar Peter, dressed as a Roman warrior, rode stirrupless, his great steed mounted on massive stone. And opposite the Michael Palace, Peter's descendant, Nicholas I, sat splendid on his war horse. I wondered that the citizens suffered them to ride so high. Moscow, I suggested to Emily, would never tolerate these proud imperial figures. "Soviet citizens do not forget their country's history," Emily replied primly. "Stal*een* says we should study the past in order that we may understand the present."

"An original thought," I replied, adding that no doubt the Kremlin made the most of it? This was the nearest I had come to open criticism. Whether for tourists or citizens, in this country of rebels, rebellion simply did not pay.

After a month in Moscow, Emily had come north with me to look for Anton Rubinstein, the Petersburger, who had accomplished for his city what his brother Nicholas had done for Moscow. Emily and I shared an enormous, brass-chandeliered bedroom in the Hotel Astoria, facing St. Isaac's Cathedral. Tsars had made this city, and from the first, I felt it to be tsar-haunted. These monumented figures gave their tone to the surroundings as the old Kremlin gave its tone to Moscow. For all its size and socialist bureaucracy, Moscow on her seven hills remains a provincial city, Slavic, intensely Russian. So it had been in Nicholas Rubinstein's day and so it appeared in 1937. Anton Rubinstein the Petersburger, Nicholas the Muscovite: their characters had differed as their cities differed — Nicholas with his easy ways, Anton with his magnificence. In Moscow, old Prince Dolgoruki, receiving Nicholas Rubinstein in the afternoons, had worn his long, brocaded Tartar dressing gown — a gesture that Petersburg would never have tolerated; imperial etiquette required of its nobility epaulets and gleaming boots. From the imperial palace down to the youngest schoolboy at the lycée, Petersburg had been a forest of uniforms. Tsarist etiquette — the strictest in Europe — had meant heel clickings and foreign bows, French ways brought in by Peter the Great and retained in society even after Napoleon's invasion had made French ways abhorred.

Muscovites, I knew, had always disliked St. Petersburg, grumbled when they had to go there and fled home as fast as train or diligence could carry them, happier on their muddy streets than walking the grand Nevsky Prospekt, with its shops that tried to look like Paris, its millinery that bore the stylish label *de Pétersbourg*. The imperial government had supported an army of clerks and subclerks, housed in apartment buildings all over the city. On the twentieth of the month these clerks received their pay; Petersburg lived, it was said, according to the "psychology of the twentieth."

"Why it iss so cold in this Gott damned Leningrad?" Emily said suddenly, one afternoon. We sat in our hotel room translating, bundled up in suits and winter overcoats, though it was early May. A damp wind blew east past Kronstadt, it seemed to penetrate one's bones. This was the first time I had heard Emily swear and I was delighted; it seemed to imply at least some recognition of God. Already in those first days Emily showed herself restless, she wanted to go home to Moscow. Then we must translate for longer hours; we must work faster, I told her, pleased that our tutelary roles seemed now to be reversed; in Moscow Emily had lectured *me*.

The moment we had stepped off the train in Leningrad, Emily's manner had changed. She talked freely, chattering and laughing. In our hotel room, when we grew stiff with sitting at translation, we threw off our coats and galoshes and Emily taught me Russian dance steps, humming, whistling, cracking her fingers expertly. The change was startling and could have no reason behind it but our distance from the Kremlin and from Emily's Intourist bosses. In times of trouble a capital city is always tense. And certainly, these were troubled times. . . . In Moscow, the night before we left, I had tried to give Emily a present, in my hotel room. It was only a bright pretty compact with a turbaned Negro boy on the lid, worth in those days perhaps a dollar. But Emily had waved it away and burst into expostulating Russian as if I were trying to bribe her. Here in Leningrad she let me present her with a fountain pen, she used my Energine for spots on her clothes. (The little tin of Energine was everywhere considered miraculous.) One morning Emily even told me shyly that she regretted the incident of the proffered compact. She made no explanation. But I was certain, by now, that my Moscow room had been wired and Emily had been afraid.

The very fact that we could do our translating in the hotel room was significant of our distance from the Kremlin and bureaucracy. In Moscow the books could not leave the libraries; our whispered translating had disturbed the other readers and we were constantly being shushed at and hissed. The Leningrad Conservatory, on the other hand, allowed us to take books home and even manuscripts. From time to time librarians telephoned to ask how I was getting along—and was there any way they could help my work? I had sat in the Conservatory library, talking with the two lady librarians, who could not seem to have enough of me. They wanted to know the state of music in America; concerning the Rubinsteins they had found no one, they said, who was so familiar with the brothers as I. The Seventy-fifth Anniversary of the Leningrad Conservatory was approaching; a booklet was being prepared about its founder, Anton Rubinstein, and every detail seemed pertinent.

I told the ladies about Anton, on tour in America in 1872, and how the Americans had loved him . . . how the New York Philharmonic Orchestra serenaded under his hotel window, and how, when Anton on the concert platform shook his mane and crashed down on the opening chords of his own D-minor Concerto, the New York audience rose as if it were mesmerized, and began to shout. I told how Anton was besieged with would-be American pupils, wrote a *Yankee Doodle Fantasia,* grew angry when the Americans said that because he was a born genius, of course he did not need to practice his instrument. . . . On tour in Chicago, Anton complained about the muddy drinking water; the citizens told him it was as nourishing as food. But in Cincinnati, Philadelphia, Boston, Detroit, when Anton arrived at his hotel room with the rented piano, he began at once to practice. . . .

The telling of it did me good, somehow. It seemed natural and right to sit in that shabby room of books and music, and talk of Anton Gregorovitch. The librarians listened starry-eyed, and in return they showed me pictures . . . photographs of Anton's villa at suburban Peterhof, with the tower room where he worked, the desk and concert grand . . . the white piano in the drawing room, the globe lamp and marble busts, the shining inlaid floors and the comfortable awnings outside in summer . . . pictures of the thatched stone house in Bessarabia where the brothers were born under the shoulder of a hill. My biography was to open, I told the librarians, with the scene of sixty Rubinsteins being baptized in the Nicholas Church at Berdichev. The boys' German mother, Clara, had planned it and carried it through. Anton, when he was an old man and famous, showed himself bitter about this baptism. A Jew was a Jew, he said, and could take pride in it. Anton must have forgotten the pogroms, I suggested to the ladies; in the time of Nicholas I, a Jew could not migrate north to Moscow nor study with hope of a musical career. Any musician, Jew or Gentile, had been a third-class citizen until Anton won for his Conservatory graduates the official title of *Free Artist*. What did the ladies think of those two words as title for my book?

While we talked, half in French, half in English, Emily sat in a corner, perfectly still. But when we left the Conservatory she stopped on a street corner and looked up at me. "You are my class enemy," she said. "But in time of peace, even enemies can be friends. Tell me, Ekaterina Genrichovna, what do you think of me?"

In Moscow she would never have put such a question. I was touched, disarmed and no doubt I showed it. Next day I went alone to the Conservatory to meet the Director, Maximilian Steinberg, and to watch the violin teaching. Emily said that she might join me later, but she did not come. For three hours I went from room to room with Steinberg in blissful freedom, politics forgotten, feeling myself much at home. The place was like all musical conservatories that I had known. I saw bare rooms, uncarpeted and resonant, each with its battered grand piano, a boy or girl playing violin or cello, a teacher astride a chair or walking up and down, smoking a cigarette, beating time. "I love to teach," Anton Rubinstein had said. "I, who to concert audiences am mad and impatient, I can sit for hours — so long as there is a spark to fan to life. I say to pupils, 'The problem is not so much how to execute these notes. How does it *sound?* That is the question. Listen, listen to yourselves!'" He had told his piano pupils not to think in terms of percussion but to sing the melody — sing it aloud. Then they would see for themselves how to phrase, where to breathe.

Walking the corridor I noted glass doors to several of the teaching rooms. I remarked on it, smiling, and said I recalled the turmoil in Moscow when Nicholas Rubinstein had installed glass doors in his Conservatory. Teachers, the world over, are inclined to fall in love with pupils, or vice versa — a phenomenon that induces pupils to practice harder, but at times brings other complications. I too, I said, at seventeen had fallen hopelessly in love with my violin teacher, a Dutchman of some fifty summers.

It was a trivial observation; the fact that I could make it showed our remoteness from the Kremlin. Here in Leningrad a little frivolity was not frowned on; nor did Maximilian Steinberg animadvert concerning socialist aims, or music as an instrument of "progress." The Moscow Conservatory walls had been hung with placards addressed to the "musical workers," slogans of exhortation that confused melody with socialism and art with propaganda. Also, in their Director's room I had noted a large bronze bust of Marshal Voroshilov, an even larger bust of Lenin — and in a corner, a shabby little bust of Beethoven, so small I had to cross the room to recognize who it was. These items and effects had not, I suppose, done harm to Moscow music teaching or marred the excellence of student performance; the Moscow concerts had proved it. For me however these things had altered some elemental proportion, banishing all harmony and ease.

Here in Leningrad I saw music taught for its own sake, and I was happy at the sight and sound. I watched a violin teacher, himself a pupil of the great Auer. Aidlin, I think his name was. The boy he taught was playing the slow movement of the Mendelssohn Concerto. He was a plump boy, perhaps thirteen years old. Red-faced from exertion, he stood with feet wide apart, rooted to the floor. In this room the resonance was cruel, each slightest fault exposed. *"Vot! Da!"* said Aidlin. ". . . Two, three. One *two* three." He took the violin from his pupil and spoke to me in English. "Too much *forces,"* he said. In rapid Russian he talked to his pupil and then turned back to me. "I tell this boy he is red in the face from trying. This music must stand alone. He should not try to help the music. I tell him I am blind — I must *hear* this music, yes? He must make me hear it." Aidlin set the instrument under his chin and played the passage in question, perhaps twelve measures. The melody emerged clear, strong — and light as breath.

"If I could come here as a pupil," I asked Aidlin wistfully, "would you teach me?" Aidlin smiled, Steinberg smiled; we shook hands all round.

Emily and I stayed only ten days in Leningrad. In all my years of experience as a biographer, I think I never found my material so quickly nor made so direct a transition from the present to the past. Actually it was not I who accomplished this magic. Simply, the scenes were before me and spoke in terms of their own authority. This was a city of bridges, of canals, deltas and reclaimed marshland. Through it the river Neva ran like a wide street. Standing on the riverbank I saw the islands, still tree-covered and pleasant as they had been in Anton Rubinstein's day. On these islands the nobility had had their summer villas. Rubinstein's patron and friend, the Grand Duchess Helena Pavlovna, had lived on Kammenoy Island, and there Anton had lived too, in summer, as her *Kapellmeister*. "Palace Janitor for Music," Anton called himself. He had been twenty-two years old, very handsome and dashing. His duties were to compose waltzes for the young ladies to dance to in the evenings, songs and little operas for them to sing. Each fortnight he had fallen romantically in love with another young princess. Some say indeed that Anton was Helena Pavlovna's lover. A doubtful surmise, yet Anton adored her and all her life she helped him with his plans; but for Helena Pavlovna, Anton could not have founded his Conservatory. Here on the enchanted island, Rubinstein had written his maligned and much loved *Kammenoy Ostrov,* and his *Melody in F.* From his chamber window he could see, on white summer nights, the warships lying at anchor by Kronstadt fortress, where the Bay widens to the Baltic Roads.

On Vasilyevsky Island the red brick buildings of the University rose behind the trees. In Rubinstein's day the floating bridges were taken up in winter; his students crossed the ice on planks to hear the University concerts. Westward the two old lighthouses, wooden and peaked, to me looked very Norse and Finnish. Sailors walked along the quay; sailors indeed were everywhere. They clustered in groups on the steps of public buildings or by Tsar Peter's statue to have their pictures taken by their shipmates. They passed me now, red-cheeked and sturdy, the ribbons from their round hats blowing.

Upriver the Fortress of St. Peter and St. Paul rose grim behind its drawbridge, within its walls the Cathedral spire flashed against a sullen sky. The last political prisoner was released in 1924, but the fortress has a bloody history of assassination, floggings to death and men gone mad from solitary confinement. Behind its walls I saw the flimsy structure of a scenic railway, put up to amuse the proletariat, and in this setting incongruous as a dream. Along the river the trees were budding; now in early May the birches showed their delicate pale green. But the air was harsh, the sunlight fitful and in the mornings fog rolled in from the Baltic. Anton Rubinstein had fled this climate to Italy when possible. To dry his damp Petersburg bones, he said. The squares were still paved handsomely with wooden blocks, small, set diamond-wise. Though I knew the principal tsarist streets by name, I could not find them, they were changed as in Moscow, since the revolution. The old Senate Square had become Decembrist Square, named for that first tragic attempt at rebellion, long ago. The Nevsky Prospekt was now the Prospekt of the Twenty-fifth of October — as hopeless a project in nomenclature, I thought, as changing New York's Sixth Avenue to Avenue of the Americas. Wars and revolutions notwithstanding, what citizen can take time for such pronouncements?

I walked the streets of this great city like a person in a trance . . . St. Isaac's was a showpiece of cathedral gloom; I was lost among the mammoth granite pillars, the tall columns of Siberian lapis lazuli, the malachite that gleamed bright jeweled green. In the great Kazan Cathedral, red flags were furled above the altar, and at the altar's depth, where once the cross had been, stood Lenin's bust in marble. At Tsarkoe Selo, the Empress Catherine had lined her rooms of state with shining silver, solid walls of it, or of carved amber — barbaric, rich, incredible. In the Michael Palace, where all one winter Anton Rubinstein had lived as Helena Pavlovna's Janitor of Music, I saw from a marble hallway the staircase sweep upward in wide arms, ornamented with malachite vases, tall as a man. Star-decked generals, stiff with etiquette, had walked these polished floors, their ladies on their arms, while outside their coachmen waited round the bonfires, dressed in furred coats and huge cocked hats. Anton had played often in the great salon upstairs. Tsar Nicholas I had sat behind him, asking for such and such a song, whistling the tunes and tapping time with his foot. The Grand Duke Michael, Helena Pavlovna's husband, had been bored with any music beyond the fashionable Italian light opera. He had disciplined the officers of his guard by making them sit through Glinka's operas, and when Liszt came to town, Duke Michael had inquired in French if it were one of Liszt's bad jokes, to insist that Glinka was a genius?

I saw the Salle de la Noblesse, once a stately glitter of white and gold, its ballroom flanked by a splendid colonnade of pillars. I saw the Winter Palace, where in Anton's day the white-walled rooms had mirrored the dazzle of twenty thousand wax tapers. Outside the ballroom doors the Tsar's grenadiers, gigantic men in bearskin hats, had stood to guard Majesty while it danced. When Anton first played in Petersburg as a boy, a *Wunderkind,* he had been much impressed with the Tsar's forty uniformed horn players. Each man had but one note to blow and timed it perfectly. To the ears of Majesty the effect was gorgeous and outdid the most splendid organ.

What I saw was only the shell, the shards and husks of imperial splendor. But still I saw it, and even in decay it had its eloquence. The Neva was bordered for perhaps a quarter-mile with what had once been ducal palaces. Over their doors the stone lintels were decorated with the imperial eagle, painted gorgeously in carmine, black and gold. Now the eagles were broken and defaced; one could see where the Comrades had torn at them in fury. I pointed out the sight to Emily, and her nostrils spread angrily. "The eagle!" she said. "Did you not see the partisans stamp upon it, last night at the ballet?"

I had seen it indeed, and would not soon forget the sight. In a spectacle entitled *Partisan Days,* the entire male *corps de ballet,* dressed in boots and hairy Cossack cloaks, had snatched the imperial flag from its place and danced upon it, uttering sharp musical cries of triumph. By invitation, Emily and I had shared a box with Vaganova, the celebrated ballerina, and six Spanish sailors from the civil war, who had been brought here, they told me frankly, as propaganda. It was the first time the ballet corps had come down off their famous points and executed folk dances on the balls of their feet. Vaganova said they had been extremely nervous as to the result, especially the gliding Georgian movement, where the women run across stage without rising an inch between steps. The girls had almost mutinied. Classic ballet has nothing approaching that step; the girls had been trained for years to certain routine postures. They said what a humiliation it would be if the Leningrad Ballet, with its famous technique, should fail in a step that every Georgian peasant woman could do. And they had failed, said Vaganova, until Vainonen, the choreographer, imported a peasant girl from the Caucasus to teach them.

Partisan Days had been performed at the old Mariensky Theater — of all buildings that I entered, for me the most nostalgic. Small and intimate, it was the perfect setting for Tchaikovsky's operas, for Rubinstein's ballets or the fairy tales of Rimsky-Korsakov. There I had seen *Swan Lake* performed, *The Sleeping Beauty, Russalka,* and the *Fairy Tale of the Tsar Saltan.* The Mariensky Theater included, when I was there, not one sign or symbol of Marxism. Downstairs the seats were comfortable armchairs, upholstered in damask, which the years had faded to a delicious blue. Above the boxes the draped curtains were charmingly tasseled, and around a crystal chandelier, painted nymphs pranced elegantly across the ceiling. In the foyer stood a handsome bust of Anton Rubinstein, looking young and vigorous, flanked by Mozart on the one side and Wagner on the other. Anton had hated Richard Wagner and all his works. But Anton had loved fame and the recognition of his countrymen. He would surely have admired this sight of himself between two such giants.

Partisan Days had featured mass scenes with the red banner flying. Twenty abreast the victorious partisans marched downstage, singing their hearts out against a rolling backdrop of the sky in flames. It was purest corn, it was George M. Cohan all over again and it shook me to the bone, reducing me to tears and shouting. My reaction had pleased Vaganova, who inquired why I, a woman from a capitalist country, wept at this drama of the Russian Revolution? "Because it's a good show!" I told her. "Because it's good theater!" Vaganova had laughed and nodded her assent, but Emily had been provoked. "This ballet is no pretty fairy tale," she told me. "It is a true story altogether. It is the story of our glorious socialist uprising."

After the freedom of Leningrad, I dreaded the return to Moscow with all its ideological frustrations. But when I arrived at the hotel bureau, Intourist greeted me with actual cordiality. During our absence, it seemed that I had been in demand. Comrade Rukavishnikov, Curator of the Tchaikovsky Museum at Klin, had come to Moscow to discover the whereabouts of Madame Boyen. In his hand he carried my biography of Tchaikovsky. He had had letters about me, he said, and had been expecting me for weeks. Why, he asked indignantly, had Madame Boyen not telephoned to Klin?

This recital, so unexpected and delightful, went instantly to my head and I came near to ruining everything by reminding Intourist that if they had been willing to listen instead of insulting me, they would have known about all this two months ago, the day of my arrival. . . . Emily was standing by me at the desk; I felt her foot on mine, pressing it sharply. I drew a long breath and let it out. "Thank you very much, sir," I said. "When can Intourist organize a tour to Klin?" It was already arranged, they told me, smiling. At Klin station a *drozhka* would meet us and drive us, tomorrow, to Tchaikovsky's house near Maidanovo. Comrade Rukavishnikov expected us.

We set out for Klin on a morning of miserable rain and cold. The town is a two hours' ride on the direct railway line to Leningrad. We were alone in our compartment and Emily amused herself by playing what we had come to call "the game." Altogether of Emily's creation, the game had been invented in Leningrad. It began by Emily asking me what time her ship was due in New York? Quite early in the morning, I would reply. Early enough for us to go shopping all day on Fifth Avenue, before the cocktail parties began at six P.M., after which we must dress for dinner at Mrs. Cornelius Vanderbilt's. "Shall I wear my evening gown?" Emily would say. "The black velvet one, down to here and here?" — pointing to her bosom, then her shoes. Yes, I would say; down to there and there. But didn't she think ice-blue satin would be more becoming, with her eyes and hair?

"And shall I go to the millionaire capitalist houses, and dance with the millionaires?"

Yes, I would say again. "But only with the young, beautiful millionaires. Not with the old wicked ones who exploit the workers."

Emily could not have enough of it. Along Fifth Avenue we shopped for cocktail dresses, high-heeled shoes, lingerie and flowery hats. At first she had tried to confuse the issue by asking if I would invite my colored handyman, Howard, to dine with us at Mr. Vanderbilt's. In some connection I once had mentioned Howard, and Emily had never let him go; his name was invitation for an ideological discussion in which she came out inevitable victor. After I told her I would not play the game unless she left out Howard, I heard no more about him. "Will my partner bow to me, in the ballroom — so?" Emily would ask. "And what shall I do then, shall I take his arm?" She was a wonderful mimic, all her gestures were valid and graceful. "Will my partner wear white kid gloves to dance with me, and shall I put my diamond bracelets *outside* my long gloves, like this?" Yes, I would say gravely. "It would be a pity to cover them up."

There was never any conclusion to the game, and of course, no moral. In due time Emily would simply stop talking, stare ahead of her for awhile and return to her role as guide. I wondered, sometimes, if the game had had its origin in my frank grumbling at the manners of the Comrade workers. I had told her I could see neither patriotism nor good Marxism in shoving me through tramcars until I stumbled and fell, or darting through doors ahead of a lady and then slamming the door in her face. ("How do you get out of tramcars in your own country?" Emily had asked.) Always, she defended her countrymen, though I reminded her that I had met her *babushka,* and her *babushka's* manners were as good as anybody's.

But it was a trifle ironic that when the *drozhka* deposited us at Tchaikovsky's gate, we were met by a gentleman whose manners could not have been bettered in any time or place. Rukavishnikov was a man in his fifties, who spoke beautiful French, and no English. "I do not understand French," Emily whispered. "So you will be able to talk freely."

Before I could digest the full portent of this, we were in Tchaikovsky's house, Rukavishnikov had bowed us through the living room door and I was enveloped in a haze of nostalgic pleasure. . . . Here was the work table on which Tchaikovsky had written his Sixth Symphony. Here was his Becker piano, a score standing on the rack. I saw manuscripts of the *Sleeping Beauty* ballet and the *Nutcracker Suite,* written in pencil, much scribbled over and altered by the

composer. The walls were hung with photographs of Tchaikovsky's family: his brothers Modest and Anatol, his nephews
and the beloved Davidov nieces, pretty young women in long
skirts, their hair piled high, smiling and preening at the
camera. Tchaikovsky's laurel wreaths were faded and dusty
behind glass; the house was cold but the rooms were light,
and outside in the little garden there were flowers.

I followed Rukavishnikov upstairs — he took them two at
a time like a boy. Up here was no museum dust and glass,
but the naked startling presence of things past. Tchaikovsky's
bed was narrow; on a nail beside it hung his dressing gown.
The closet door was open. I saw Tchaikovsky's hats on the
shelf — a black fedora, a flat straw hat, a high gray felt that
looked very elegant, like Ascot, and surprisingly, four high
silk hats. The dressing table was petticoated; on it were no
less than ten bottles of perfume — Guerlain's *Caprice,* Bey
Rhum, a bottle of hair tonic with an inch of liquid still
remaining. Hatboxes stood on the floor, and a little traveling
trunk, ready for instant flight. "Where will Peter Ilich go
next?" I asked Rukavishnikov. "To Brailov for a visit with
Nadejda von Meck? To Florence with his brother Anatol?
To Cambridge, England, to receive that last degree of Doctor
of Music?"

It was an extraordinary intimacy, here in the little bedroom; I felt myself an intruder. "One should knock at
this door before entering," I told Rukavishnikov. He smiled
and led me downstairs. We had tea at the dining room table
from a big samovar, then sat in the living room and talked
until four, when we dined on steaming bowls of delicious
potato soup, made with sour cream, followed by fish and black
bread. We were a company of six: Rukavishnikov, Emily,

myself, the Klin telegraph operator and an attractive girl student from the Moscow Conservatory who boarded in the house. At five the *drozhka* returned for us — an open victoria with the same dilapidated peasant driver. Rukavishnikov kissed my hand in farewell, bowed to Emily and we embarked for the station, a mile and a half away. Literally embarked, the rain came down in torrents.

Wet through, chilled to the bone, we boarded in due time the local train for Moscow and sat in the hard cars with crowds of peasants playing accordions and singing, most of them happily drunk. Tomorrow was Rest Day. "Saturday night," I remarked to Emily, "is the same in every country." One old farmer, dressed in blouse and ragged felt boots, was helped — or ejected — from the train by a young soldier. Dropping on his knees the drunken man shuffled after the embarrassed soldier down the length of the platform, his hands pointed as if in prayer, babbling drunken sentences. Plainly, he was begging not to be punished. And plainly, the young soldier had no such intentions and desired only to be rid of him. The entire car, stationed at the windows, watched this tableau, roared with laughter and offered advice. As the train pulled out I saw the soldier break into a run, fleeing his tormentor. . . .

This performance had been far from Emily's taste. The suggestion of fear on the part of the old peasant, his abject prayers to authority had held perhaps too much of tsarism and too little of the socialist heaven I was supposed to see. I was, Emily informed me at that point, the only American that had been permitted to go to Klin in the past five years. For this I was grateful, I replied. "And besides," I added, "we have drunken people in America, and they do not sing half so well as the Comrades." I waved toward the car, which again had burst into a stomping, rollicking ballad. The windows were shut, the stench was awful and so were the fleas.

There was a long silence, after which Emily remarked that Comrade Rukavishnikov was a handsome old man. "He bowed to me," she said. "He opened the door and let me pass first." Monsieur Rukavishnikov, I replied, was a gentleman. Old-fashioned, like myself, I added — and perhaps like Emily's grandfather? Emily shook her head. Patently, her grandfather was made of other stuff than Rukavishnikov. "But these beautiful old-fashioned manners," I persisted, "they do no harm to anyone? Or do they?"

Emily shook her head again. She spoke slowly, thoughtfully. "No, Ekaterina Genrichovna," she said. "They do no harm."

On the Pripet marshes the sun was hot, the horse chestnut trees in bloom; their white fluff drifted fragrant at the railroad stations. Everywhere were flowers, big and bright and lavish. Before leaving Russia I had traveled down to Kiev alone, sans Emily. The Rubinsteins were southern born, I needed a glimpse of this lush country where the peonies grew big as basketballs and there was no such word as fog. The Dnieper banks were sandy and on the high bluffs above I saw the ancient monastery, its golden towers gleaming. Here the family Rubinstein, traveling by covered wagon, had halted on its journey northward from Berdichev. Anton was only five at the time, but he remembered. The deep voices of the monastery bells had followed the caravan around a last turning in the forest road. Anton's mother had looked back. "Farewell, Mother Kiev," she said.

I saw the monastery domes and knew that my journey was over.

"How was it?" Madame von Meck asked me, in New York. "How was it in Moscow? How was it for you, and how is it now, in my poor country?"

I made some quick, conventional reply. Could I explain Emily to this woman of another time, another ethos? Could I explain Moscow as I had seen it, and Leningrad? I thought of the red banners furled in the Kazan Cathedral, of Lenin's bust at the altar's depth . . . the *Internationale* at midnight from the Kremlin chimes . . . the Peter and Paul Fortress with the scenic railway against its walls . . . the eagle defaced, the Comrades fingering the malachite vases in the Michael Palace. I thought of the question Madame von Meck had asked in the beginning — if I would lose, in the U.S.S.R., my hard-won perspective, my feeling of familiarity with the nineteenth-century scene.

I shook my head. "The ghost of Anton Rubinstein walks strong in Petersburg," I said. "The Baltic fog rolls in along the Neva. I saw it snake around the pillars of the Admiralty building and blot out Tsar Peter on his horse. In Moscow, Nicholas Gregorovitch still haunts the streets by his Conservatory. In the country the birch trees are beautiful, and I saw women plowing barefoot in the snow. . . . But I wouldn't go there if I were you," I told Madame von Meck. "Not if they stamped your passport in gold. I think that it would break your heart to see it."

3

On Interviewing and Evidence: Boston and Holmes

The title came to me long afterward, when the book was finished: *Yankee from Olympus*. At the moment, I knew only that I was going to write about Holmes —Justice Oliver Wendell Holmes of the United States Supreme Court. "O. W. H., Jr.," Boston called him in his younger days, when his father, the brave little doctor of five feet three, still overtopped his son in fame.

This time, I was writing about my own country, and a man dead only five years since. By these tokens the work should prove easier than my biographies of Tchaikovsky and the brothers Rubinstein. There would be no tedious translating from the Russian, no hazardous crossing of far-flung borderlands by dead of night. And more than that, no bearding of institutional directors and hostile tourist bureaus, no rebuffs from the political frontier. True, Holmes had been a lawyer and my training lay in music, not the law. Yet when

I took the lawbooks from the shelf and read Holmes's representative opinions and his great dissents, they were neither obscure nor incomprehensible. *"The Fourteenth Amendment does not enact Mr. Herbert Spencer's Social Statics — our Constitution is an experiment, as all life is an experiment. . . . Free thought — not free thought for those who agree with us but freedom for the thought that we hate."*

Here was nothing specialized, esoteric, to be received and cherished only by the guild of legal scholars. Here, on the contrary, was a part of one's heritage, one's birthright as an American. I was writing about a lawyer, true enough. But I was writing also about a great man, and great men have a way of breaking free from professional boundaries and professional cliques. The history books had it that Holmes, with his later colleagues, the Justices Brandeis and Cardozo, was concerned with something called "sociological jurisprudence." Holmes put it more simply. "The life of the law," he said, "has not been logic but experience, and the rules by which men should be governed have been determined not by syllogism but by the felt necessities of the time."

Holmes's friend, John Chipman Gray, who taught forty-odd years at the Harvard Law School, went further and remarked that constitutional law was not law but politics. Like most epigrams, this was to be received with caution, yet at least it pointed to the truth. For me there was deep satisfaction in dealing at last with the history of my own country. For six years I had studied Europe and Russia, their annals, politics, music, culture. I knew about the German Revolution of 1848 but not about Mr. Madison's War of 1812; I could describe the personality and character of Czar Alexander III, but not General Grant or Grover Cleveland.

From my study walls I took down the maps of Moscow and Bessarabia. Pictures of Boston and Cambridge replaced them; maps of the United States in 1841 when Holmes was born and in the year 1800, with the states isolated along the Atlantic waters.

Holmes's story, it soon became plain, included not only a hero but a protagonist: the United States of America. Every biography is in essence a "life and times"; with Holmes it was especially true. The stamp of his inheritance lay on him; boy and man, he took his spiritual sustenance from Boston, Cambridge, New England. No matter if one wrote of him as a soldier in the Civil War, wounded three times, or as a teacher of law and a judge, contemplative, seemingly remote, Holmes's fate and the business of his life seemed tied to his country, inseparable from it. "It is required of a man," he said, "that he must share the action and passion of his time at peril of being judged never to have lived."

In the writing of biography, it is expedient to approach one's subject from the periphery, from the outside in — to study first the times, then move to the localities and persons of the immediate story. This is true especially when the biographer shifts, as I have done, from century to century and from continent to continent. With Holmes it was first of all necessary to know the great names, the movers and shakers at the White House, in Congress and the law courts; to be familiar with them as one is familiar with names in newspapers of today and with current controversial events. Now at the outset of work I roamed and read in blissful desultory fashion: old histories like Woodrow Wilson's and James Ford Rhodes's; McLaughlin's *Constitutional History,* Washburn's *Sketches of the Judicial History of Massachu-*

setts, Frankfurter on Holmes, Cardozo on *Law and Literature,* Moses Aronson on juridical evolutionism. I read
biographies and letters of Theodore Roosevelt, Mark Hanna
and the political bosses. Even the *Federalist* papers must be
reread, though I could not hope to encompass them with any
thoroughness. I bought books by the dozen and the score and
kept them by, where I could make notes on margins and
endboards; the twenty-six volumes of my *Dictionary of
American Biography* bristled with paper markers. I read at
mealtime and I read in bed — not as a scholar reads, in order
to form new judgments on fresh-discovered material, but as
a reporter might read, to learn the background of the scenes
I must depict.

It was a comfort, in these vasty beginnings, to think of
oneself as a historical reporter; the notion brought one's
project within reasonable limits. It was a comfort also when
this national story began to reduce itself to Massachusetts
boundaries. At the university library I followed down the list
of books Holmes studied at the Harvard Law School in 1867.
Most of them, as I read along, were positively repellent, and
I figured that Wendell Holmes, when first he opened them,
was as green as I. Henry James had left the Law School
because he could not understand, he wrote, a word of what
the books said or what the lecturer said. Holmes also hesitated. "One saw that artists and poets shrank from the law
as from an alien world. One doubted oneself how it could
be worthy the interest of an intelligent mind." A few of the
books were readable for the layman, like Walker's *Introduction to American Law,* which Holmes said he enjoyed because it gave him a sense of legal historical continuity.

Soon, when I knew enough to feel easy in the nineteenth-century scene, I could sally forth and talk to people. In Washington, Justice Holmes employed a new law secretary each year, bright young men sent down from Harvard, culled from the graduating crop by Professor Felix Frankfurter. Many of these had since attained high place in government and business. On the list I ticked off twelve for interviewing. I did not choose them because they were Attorney Generals of the United States or Chairman of the Board of U. S. Steel, but because they had served at some key point of Holmes's career, such as the year Mrs. Holmes died and Holmes wrote, in the week after her death, his great dissent in the Rosika Schwimmer case.

Experience told me I would not get from these men, or indeed from any interview, the larger aspect of Holmes, or any significant information about the celebrated dissents and representative opinions. These things were in the books, discussed ad infinitum, for and against. Nor would I have dreamed of interviewing anybody until I knew the great cases (and the lesser) as a historical reporter might know them, together with the circumstances of national expediency that had brought the litigations forward.

And the more I learned about Oliver Wendell Holmes, Jr., the more insupportable it became to think of him as dead, cold and motionless beneath that stone at Arlington. I found myself possessed by a witch's frenzy to ungrave this man, stand him upright, see him walk, jump, dance, tell jokes, make love, display his vanity or his courage as the case might be. National encomium, the laying on of laurels had only buried him deeper. The difficulty was to uncover material that gave proof of life — not noble public posture but characteristic brief turns of phrase, small oddities and manners that belonged to Holmes and to Holmes alone. Especially I must find material about the young Holmes. Justice Holmes of the United States Supreme Court, ninety-four at death, was remembered everywhere as a "magnificent old man." The phrase offended me. What I looked for was the brilliant judge of forty-odd in Massachusetts, the young Harvard graduate in the wide-awake hat, on his shoulder the star of the Twentieth Regiment, Massachusetts Volunteers.

Men and women existed by the score who had talked with Justice Holmes. In Boston there were grandfathers who had even known Holmes's father, the Doctor, "Autocrat of the Breakfast Table." By now I was aware that my book must open early, long before Holmes's birth in 1841 — perhaps with his father's birth in 1809, or with some scene introducing Holmes's grandfather, the Reverend Mr. Abiel Holmes of Holmes Place, Cambridge, who wrote the first comprehensive annals of his country. An Oliver Wendell Holmes was not, after all, a Tchaikovsky, a man *sui generis,* who would have fulfilled his genius in any place or time. With these Holmeses the generations intertwined, their roots went deep into New England soil.

I read Abiel Holmes's *Annals of America* and was charmed by them. Abiel wrote of the United States as a man who is in the midst of history. . . . *"The president sent captains Lewis and Clarke to explore the river Missouri. . . . The Lehigh coal, obtained at the Mauch Chunk mountain in Pennsylvania, was brought into notice. William Trumbull had an ark constructed, which brought down 200 or 300 bushels to Philadelphia. . . . At Mr. Spalding's plantation, on Sapelo island, were made 25 lbs. of good sugar, and the next year, 84 lbs."*

Whatever Abiel set down, each word was instinct with pride in his country's growth. I went through Dr. Holmes's novels, one by one, and his essays, his brave treatise on "The Contagiousness of Puerperal Fever"; his poems, printed in two stout volumes. What extraordinary verse! Poured out by the hatful, the bucketful, sentimental, patriotic, religious, written for banquets or birthdays or for young men marching to war — and always lively, evocative of the time and the occasion. *America to Russia,* wrote the good Doctor, in 1866, celebrating the visit of a Grand Duke:

> *A nation's love in tears and smiles*
> *We bear across the sea,*
> *O Neva of the banded isles,*
> *We moor our hearts in thee!*

A strange mooring indeed; one could hardly believe it, all things considered. How, I asked myself, how can one paint the past except through the coloration of the present, of today and today's ethos? It would be an immense help to talk with persons who had known the Holmeses, who could recall them as they were, not as legend painted them. But where should I begin, with these interviews? Should I start with the law secretaries or with the old guard in Boston, the men and women who had known Holmes when he was young: Bishop Lawrence of Massachusetts, Mr. A. Lawrence Lowell who had been President of Harvard, Miss Katharine Loring of Pride's Crossing, Mr. and Mrs. Arthur Dehon Hill, Mr. Robert Barlow. The first three were in their eighties or nineties. It came to me that I had better hurry. The law secretaries could wait; even Beacon Hill Bostonians do not last forever.

I did not trouble with introductions but simply wrote ahead, declared my purpose and asked if I might come. (Almost everybody, I was to discover, loved to talk about their friend Justice Holmes.) Miss Loring was blind. A lady of much sweetness and dignity, she walked toward me across the polished floor of her house, on the arm of a nurse-companion. She gave me the scene of polite Boston in the eighteen-fifties and sixties — she was born in 1849. Professor Papanti's dancing class and the famous Sewing Circles, founded it was said by John Adams's daughter Abigail, "to sew for the poor." Perhaps the poor still benefited, but by Miss Loring's day the institution benefited the membership even more. The Circles were as hard to get into as the Porcellian Club; membership was an identification and a badge. Miss Loring remembered Mr. Creely, the Cambridge milkman, with his morning cans and pitcher, Mr. Brackett the butcher, who wore, she said, a spotless white coat and never smiled. She remembered the lamplighter, the old elm in the middle of Harvard Square, and Lyceum Hall where the Harvard "Coop" now stands. A big barn stood somewhere near the Square; the Harvard Assemblies were held there and they danced the cotillion. Seaver and Francis, Miss Loring said, kept a stationer's circulating library near by; she named the books they had for rental.

There was an enchantment to the way Miss Loring told it. This was Holmes's world, the world he left in July of 1861 to enlist in the Twentieth Regiment. I went from Miss Loring to Bishop Lawrence on Commonwealth Avenue, and the Bishop proved an interviewer's dream. Blue-eyed, pink-cheeked, white-haired, he walked about his study, mimicking the voices of the Holmes family, seventy years ago. He remem-

bered their houses on Beacon Street and Charles Street, he was
the one man I met who still referred to Holmes as "Wendell."
"Pitter patter all the time in that library," the Bishop said.
"Wendell's sister, 'Melia, was the only person in Boston who
could outtalk Phillips Brooks." The Bishop made me see them
all: Dr. Holmes and his wife; Wendell, Amelia and young
Neddy among the books and bric-a-brac, chattering, laughing,
bidding for attention. Wendell, he said, had a romantic
quality which the others lacked. "People felt it as soon as
they saw him, even when he was a boy."

Wendell Holmes, I knew, had attended Dixwell's Latin
School. Mr. Epes Sargent Dixwell was the father of Holmes's
future wife, Fanny, and I was interested in every detail
concerning him. It seemed a word from heaven when Bishop
Lawrence said that he too had gone to Dixwell's Latin
School. He remembered the classes, remembered also the
morning of 1865 when school let out early and bells rang
for the fall of Richmond. Mr. Dixwell, it seems, did not
dress like other proper Bostonians, in black swallowtail coat
and dark trousers but after his own taste, in purple and
green, with checked trousers, a velvet waistcoat that Benjamin
Disraeli would have fancied. True, Mr. Dixwell was color-
blind, and perhaps did not appreciate the brightness of his
plumage. "Dicky," the Bishop called him. When Dicky sat
down to read morning prayers, he took his steel-rimmed
spectacles off instead of putting them on. . . .

I emerged from 122 Commonwealth Avenue with a
high heart and a spirit warm with gratitude for the longevity
of tough, cultured Bostonians. Was it all to be as simple and
fruitful as this? Oh, let the gentlemen and ladies not die
before I could get to them! I developed a technique for inter-

viewing, very different from my past experience, which in Russia, at least, had been a matter of pushing and shoving and what might be called steely desperation. In Boston, as the days went by and one Holmes friend led to another, I did not telephone for appointments; in this atmosphere the telephone seemed a trifle abrupt. I wrote little notes to Beacon Hill addresses or State Street law offices, sent them round by Western Union messenger, then sat in my hotel and waited politely for the telephone to ring. It was tedious, but it worked.

On these excursions, I was not looking for "the law," or for the greatness of Holmes; that had been discovered elsewhere. Indeed, if I had not known Holmes's greatness and the reasons for it, I would never have ventured to these interviews. What I looked for was a way of life long vanished, the custom and ritual of another era and, incidentally, for any personal word or gesture, characteristic of the Holmeses, that I could glean. I knew of the hazards that beset those who write about the living or the recently dead: heirs, executors, relatives and friends withhold material or are lavish with it for reasons peculiarly their own. Yet in Holmes's case it had seemed to me there would be no withholding, for the reason that there was no harmful gossip to unearth. Here was a life, long and exemplary, marked by no doubtful interludes, no suicidal young women clutching photographs to their bosoms, no scandal of friendship, love or money. The pureness of it was a writer's challenge: How to interest the public in such a life? *"Les hommes heureux n'ont pas d'histoire."* I had heard it but I refused to believe it. Nor did I give much credit to Holmes's glib statement, made to a reporter, that his biography had ended in 1864, when he emerged from the Union Army.

My previous biographical heroes had been men born at the bottom of the social scale, or at best on the middle rung. By their artistry, their genius, they had climbed upward until after desperate struggle they were balanced at the peak or near it. Holmes, on the other hand, was born at the top. The inference was that he must go downward, fail to hold his father's level and the level of his father's celebrated friends and intimates: Longfellow, Lowell and the rest.

From a writer's standpoint, surely this was a "plot" worth unfolding? It implied a risk, financial as well as aesthetic, but a risk I considered well worth taking. To confess this in Boston had not occurred to me; I thought the facts of Holmes's life made the situation evident. I was taken by surprise therefore, when along Beacon Street at tea time I was queried sharply as to my motives in undertaking this biography. Did I expect to make money by it? I hoped to, I answered soberly; professional authors are accustomed to financial return from their work. There followed the word "exploit"; it was to be hoped I would not *exploit* the Judge? If the present company, I replied gloomily, could tell me how to exploit Judge Holmes, I would be happy to try. And if they could name one single American personality more difficult of exploitation, I would be surprised. Publishers had asked me to write the life of Leopold Stokowski; I had refused. Now, *there* was a name that lent itself to exploitation. But Justice Oliver Wendell Holmes? Fanny Dixwell . . . Dr. Holmes . . . Mrs. Holmes? Uncle John Holmes? The Reverend Mr. Abiel Holmes?

I had pronounced Abiel to rhyme with feel. My hearers corrected me at once. "Abile," they said, rhyming it with *while*. "In Boston, we call it Abile."

"Abile," I repeated, solemnly. There was a general look of relief and approval. But the question of exploitation came up in future visits. Holmes's will had named two of his old friends as literary executors: Mr. John Gorham Palfrey, the Boston lawyer, and Felix Frankfurter, at that time Dean of the Harvard Law School. These men controlled all letters and other personal material. On Holmes's death, it had been expected that hordes of hungry legal biographers would storm the executors' doors. Yet nearly six years had passed, I was the first to appear. And I was a foreigner from Philadelphia, a non-Bostonian, a non-lawyer and a non-man. To those concerned, it was disconcerting. Had I, the company asked, been to see John Palfrey? Had I talked with him, did I know that his daughters were the famous tennis champions?

Yes, I said; I had seen Mr. Palfrey and I had had the privilege of reading some four hundred of Holmes's unpublished letters, in Mr. Palfrey's custody. The letters had proven even more fascinating than I expected. Addressed to many different correspondents, they covered the Washington years, after 1902. I had dined with Mr. Palfrey and his agreeable wife at their house in Brookline. I did not think Mr. Palfrey was going to let me have all the material I wanted, but he had received me pleasantly and we had talked of the Holmeses at length. After dinner (I told my hearers) Mr. Palfrey had gone to his cellar and produced his best brandy. We had toasted my project, following which my host had informed me that I was wrong in thinking that his Aunt Sarah, when she was in her sixties, had ridden her tricycle around Fresh Pond in Cambridge every morning early. On the contrary, her usual course had been up and down Divinity Avenue. And if I had got my information from Colonel Higginson's book, I should know that Higginson was notoriously inaccurate.

My hearers laughed and looked pleased. I did not add that Mr. Palfrey had called Colonel Higginson an "inveterate gossip"; I was too unsure of the general bloodlines and cousinships of my audience. Old Boston, I had discovered, was riddled with feuds, hot and plainly enjoyable battles that concerned not only the living but the ancestors of the living. A little knowledgeable malice, repeated in the right direction, did wonders in opening doors and starting reminiscences. But one must be careful not to send these arrows off in the wrong direction; I seldom indulged. Nevertheless, I began to take sides and to feel Boston-domesticated. At home, they told me I was developing a Harvard accent; my *r*'s were slurred and my *a*'s not as flat as nature had made them. My clothes also underwent temporary modification. I learned not to appear on Beacon Hill doorsteps in that smart "little black dress." Tweeds were the thing, and the older the better, with a matching tweed hat, handsome suede gloves, and around the neck a discreet, unfashionable piece of fur that had belonged to my mother.

The role was not unnatural to me. Boston might look on Philadelphians as foreigners, yet Bryn Mawr and Beacon Hill are less remote than it would seem. With the gentlemen of Boston I assumed no disguises but told them briskly what I wanted, endeavoring not to waste their time. And they replied in kind. In the sprawling, two-floored law offices of Hale and Dorr were file cases containing lists of Beacon Hill inhabitants, by street and house number, covering seventy years. Mr. Richard Hale turned them over to me, together with his own map of the Holmeses' neighbors as far back as 1864. Senior member of his firm, Mr. Hale at seventy had the vigor of youth and twice its determination; he let nothing pass without full definition. When he saw that I was weak on the points of the Boston compass, Mr. Hale led me to the top of the Custom House. We walked round the roof, holding our hats and looking out to sea.

Milk Street, State Street, Joy Street, Park and Beacon, where the boy Wendell Holmes in winter had flung himself upon his sled and followed the Long Coast straight down to Washington Street or across the Common — all these I learned, step by step, trotting after Mr. Hale's long stride and wondering if all distinguished Boston lawyers wore, rain or shine, an old shapeless raincoat and squashy old felt hat. I rented an automobile and a driver, and Mr. Hale sat with me in the back, gesticulating, pointing out landmarks as we covered the road that young Abiel Holmes had taken into Boston when he migrated up from Woodstock, Connecticut. At the Boston Courthouse, Mr. Hale tracked down the questions Wendell Holmes had answered in his bar examination, March of 1867. We found the old Bar Book and photographed the page with Holmes's signature below the rest.

The Boston Medical Library on the Fenway had the pink and white seashell that inspired Dr. Holmes to write his "Chambered Nautilus." A trivial relic, on the face of it. Yet it is such things that strike spark to the biographer's tinder, that let him know his characters, prove to him that these men were not mere legend but lived through their days like the rest of us and took inspiration where they found it, in little things. The Holmes house at 296 Beacon Street was not yet dismantled; I was invited there to tea with Mr. Edward Holmes, nephew of the Justice. From his room on the third floor, Holmes as a young man had edited Kent's *Commentaries.* The famous sitting room on the second floor back, overlooking the Charles River, was almost as it had been when the family lived there. From that room, said Dr. Holmes, he looked out "on all creation," and he died there, sitting reading in his chair. A door in the wall led to a tiny lavatory. On the inside of the door hung a mirror, so low I could see only my shoulders in it. I asked Mr. Edward Holmes why the glass was set so far down. "Oh," he said, "Dr. Holmes was a very small man. He hung it for his convenience, and we have never moved it."

I had known of course that the Doctor was short. When he was a junior at Harvard he described himself as "a plumeless biped of the height of exactly five feet three inches when standing in a pair of substantial boots made by Mr. Russell of this town." Yet until I saw the mirror, it was not borne in upon me fully what the life and outlook of so small a man must be. No wonder the Doctor was cocky and strutted a bit. A man had to, whose face fitted into that low-slung piece of glass.

Of all my Boston interviews, the best, next to Bishop Lawrence, was with Mr. and Mrs. Arthur Dehon Hill, old friends of Justice Holmes and his wife, Fanny. It was Mrs. Hill who gave me my best anecdotes about Fanny Holmes. Everyone had assured me that Mrs. Holmes was quite as witty as her husband. She was original in looks, dress and speech, they said, and she made caustic remarks, quick and sharp and funny. People who knew Mrs. Holmes loved her, but she did not suffer fools gladly. Yet nobody seemed able to quote what she had said. How was a biographer to proceed? Merely to state that a woman is witty does not convince. There must be proof. It was Mrs. Hill who quoted Fanny Holmes's beautiful, desperate remark concerning the proposed move to Washington in 1902, when her husband had been named to the Supreme Court. Mrs. Holmes was a woman who had been shy, not beautiful, keeping to herself in Boston, seldom going into society, preferring to let the Judge go and shine alone. She did not dress in the prevailing fashion but in her own style, exactly as she chose. Before the move to Washington, Mrs. Hill, calling on Mrs. Holmes, had found the latter sitting alone in her little downstairs room. "Mary," said Mrs. Holmes, getting up and moving to her friend, "look at me! How can I go to Washington — I, who look like an abandoned farm in Maine?"

From that moment I "saw" Mrs. Holmes and loved her, and I was grateful. But along Beacon Street were persons of another caliber than the Hills, persons whose dispositions called for such weapons, defensive and offensive, as the interviewer could muster. There were the ladies who owned Judge Holmes, or thought they did, lock, stock and barrel. The Judge in his debonair middle age had called on these charmers in the afternoons, stopped for tea or sherry on his way down Beacon Street from the Courthouse. I did not dare neglect them; I might miss some trenchant bit, some clue to character or personality. One and all proved to be amusing talkers; Holmes was a discriminating man. The ladies were also, now in their latter days, as difficult to interview as a Russian commissar, generous one moment, suspicious the next, and, like most people who have not been in public life, inveterate enemies of the interviewer's notebook and pencil. "Oh, my dear, no no! Put that by until after lunch. Then I will send away these friends that I invited to meet you, and we can really talk."

Often enough the moment never came. Plainly, there was a flaw in my technique; the ladies were not happy with me. Perhaps it had been a mistake to introduce myself by reciting my professional qualifications as a writer; the ladies showed no interest, the conversation flagged. These were married women, possessors of large, attractive establishments. And the profession of a married woman, after all, is marriage — a taking part in the affairs of children, grandchildren, their friends and in fact all relatives down to the last cousin farthest removed. How had I overlooked this, who was reared among innumerable brothers, sister, cousins, aunts? What these scenes needed were Boston family connections of my own. As interviewer it was my business to reassure, and at once, on entrance, if possible.

At this time I had two brothers teaching at Harvard, and an aunt — Cecilia Beaux the portrait painter — who for many years had come from New York to spend the summers in her house at Gloucester, on the North Shore, above Boston. Aunt Cecilia was a friend of that redoubtable patroness of art, Mrs. Jack Gardner, who came sometimes to Gloucester for the day, or to dine. I had seen snapshots of her at tea in the loggia, smiling under her parasol, with Gloucester Bay in the distance. I trotted out Mrs. Jack, Aunt Cecilia, the two brothers and a remote grandfather who had settled in Boston (rather unsatisfactorily) in the sixteen hundreds.

The result was brilliantly successful, and well worth any discomfort it caused me. (I do not hold with this approach.) On first try, I obtained the delicious story of Mrs. Holmes's pet flying squirrels, how she insisted upon keeping them in the bedroom at Beverly Farms and how they annoyed the Judge by jumping on his bed at night. The lady who gave me the story had greeted me, on my arrival, with lips as tight as if they were carved. She had sat unbending until I produced Aunt Cecilia, when her face broke and she looked at me, astonished. "But I knew Miss Beaux quite well!" she said. "Your aunt? Oh, my dear child, I had no notion . . . Wait! Put down your coat. Don't go, I have all the time in the world. Let me run to my room and fetch some photographs. . . ."

I did not blame these ladies; indeed, I liked them. They were bright, quick, always kind about the Judge's memory and not so kind about each other, which made it only the spicier. They did well to be reserved; there was no reason they should trust the outlander, the foreigner from south of the border. Occasionally, however, they repeated each other's stories, and not always with the same slant. Like all clever talkers, the Judge, when he made a good retort, did not hoard it but contrived to use it generously. Sometimes the stories crossed, and I was troubled. Hearsay evidence — in law the court rejects it. Yet this was not hearsay but quotation at first hand. And if a conflict of quotations robbed me of certain words of Holmes's, at least it taught me much about the ladies who did the quoting.

4

Washington and Holmes

Always, during the first year's study for a biography, I have the pleasing illusion that someone will come forward and rescue me, reveal my characters as they were and lift me from the pit of doubt. Some papa, some Santa Claus of biographers will materialize, one fine day, and tell me surely what I want to know. With Holmes in particular I had this illusion. So many people lived who had known him, and each one so ready to talk!

What actually appeared, this time, was not a savior at all, but an added hazard: the "definitive" biographer was chosen by Holmes's two literary executors, Mr. Palfrey and Justice Frankfurter. It was Mr. Palfrey who told me about it. Stimulated by my researches, he said, they had named one of Holmes's law secretaries, who had been with Holmes at his death: Mark Howe, of Harvard. Mark was at war, he would not be able to work on the book for some time. But the written material, the letters I had seen would of course be reserved *in toto* for this definitive work. I must not use them, even to establish chronology or to tell me where Holmes was at a given time.

Great hopes lay in the executors' choice, Mr. Palfrey added genially. Did I not agree that it was an excellent arrangement? It was indeed, I replied politely. My head spun, there was a roaring in my ears that was not State Street traffic. I told Mr. Palfrey that I knew Mark Howe's father, Mr. Mark Antony DeWolfe Howe, a most enchanting old literary gentleman who was himself the author of some forty books and who had been a friend of my father's long ago. Here in Boston, Mr. Howe had talked much with me about Holmes and writing; I had seen his son's photograph. A handsome young lawyer, in Malta at the moment, at some wartime post of military government.

I left Mr. Palfrey's office and walked uphill toward Boston Common, by myself. So I was Lilith, outlawed from Paradise. I must pick all my flowers outside the garden; I could not pass that State Street angel with the flaming sword. Did the executors, I wondered suddenly, expect me to give up, stop work, break the contract with my publishers and simply leave the field? The question brought me up short. I think I stood stock still, there on Milk Street; I remember that a woman stopped and asked me the way to S. S. Pierce's store as if I were an inhabitant. *Perce's,* she pronounced it.

Mr. Palfrey had not tried to prevent me from writing my book. He had indeed declared his desire to help in any way he could, short of his official responsibilities as executor. I must see Tom Corcoran in Washington, he had suggested, shaking my hand in farewell. Tom had truly loved the Judge. And besides, Tom had an Irish way of looking at things, he would be a good hand at a description.

Outlawed, placed politely beyond the pale. Yet there were flowers worth picking outside those walls. And is a flower less bright for being called a weed? . . . Stop work? Of course not, the notion was shocking and somehow ridiculous. I knew what I must do. Every incident from the letters that I wanted to use, I must go out and obtain newly from a man or woman who had been part of the incident described. If I could not quote the epistolary description of, say, Holmes's eightieth birthday party — or more seriously, of his last illness and death — I must find a man who had been present and would tell me about it. The task was not impossible. The letters that I had read concerned the years 1902–1935; living witnesses were to be found in Washington and New York.

But I felt a new sense of urgency. This Mark Howe, handsome and definitive on his island of Malta, might even now be blocking out his chapters, in mind if not on paper. My book must appear first, before the *definitive* work was on the stands. The word dogged me. What, actually, did it mean? I began to think carefully about biographical evidence, I was forced to think about it. Were letters, after all, the best proof of fact, and must a thing be written down, to be true? A letter from Justice Holmes, signed by his hand, would seem to be historical evidence of the first water. Yet, evidence of what, I asked myself — of the facts mentioned in the letter, or of the writer's character? My biography of Tchaikovsky had been based almost entirely upon letters; I was used to relying on them. I remembered however that Tchaikovsky himself had not trusted letters as evidence. (And no wonder — he could write to his patroness, Nadejda von Meck, describing an incident in graceful, animated fashion, then turn round and tell the same story to his brother Anatol in

terms of boredom and disgust.) "It seems to me letters are
not perfectly sincere — I am judging by myself. No matter
to whom I am writing, I am always conscious of the effect
of my letter, not only upon the person to whom it is addressed,
but upon any chance reader. Consequently I embroider. I often
take pains to make the tone of a letter simple and sincere —
at least to make it *appear* so. But apart from letters written
at the moment when I am worked upon, I am never quite
myself in my correspondence. These letters are to me a source
of repentance, and often of agonizing regret. When I read
the correspondence of great men, published after their death,
I am always disturbed by a vague sense of insincerity and
falsehood."

Tchaikovsky had been unusual in possessing a quite
marvelous objectiveness about himself; perhaps his was the
artist's honesty, which knows that truth can be a matter of
presentation rather than of pure fact. I looked up *evidence*
in the dictionary. "That which furnishes proof," it said: "An
outward sign, an indication." I looked up *hearsay*. "Rumor,"
said Webster. "Common talk: evidence which rests in part
on the veracity of some person other than the witness." I
thought of old Sir Edward Coke in England, who would
not believe anything unless he read it. *"Non lego non credo,"*
he said.

I sought out the historians; the best of them approached
the problem boldly. "Everything," said Collingwood, "is
evidence which the historian can use as evidence." I went to
the poets, to the literary men, and was charmed to find that
Goethe had entitled his autobiography *Imagination and Truth.*
"Because," he said, "a fact in our life is important not when
it is true, but when it is meaningful." I recalled that as a

young woman I had been discouraged by the printed bibliographies that follow books of history, with sources differentiated carefully as *Primary* or *Secondary*. It was a reasonable arrangement, but somehow limiting. Suppose one's aim in writing biography is not to unearth new material, but rather to introduce one's subject to the general reader? Evocation is not a mining operation but an exercise in achieving effect. I found it refreshing, during all this, to copy and tack above my writing table Thomas Fuller's words, from his *Holy State:* "Let him die without pity, who will not quench his thirst at the river, because he cannot come in at the fountain."

In Washington, Justice Holmes's friends had included the great and the famous; I must see and talk with them if I could. Not only had I to corroborate the forbidden letters, but I was still searching for detail. By now I had enough data to describe Holmes to the age of sixty, when he left Boston. I had it from the Lawrences, the Lowells, the Lorings, the Hills, the Hales, the Barlows. But the subject of a biography cannot remain at one age — at fifty, at twenty-five, at forty. He must grow old and the reader must see and feel the process. It is not easy to describe a person, even a living man or woman whom one has seen an hour ago. Few people are able to do it convincingly. "He is jolly," they say. "He is tall . . . he is serious . . . he is very funny, in fact he is a *scream,* he had us in stitches." But they do not give details that make one see and hear the living creature.

It must be my care to spy out and find this aging, ageless Holmes. I went to New York and Washington and talked with the twelve secretaries, one by one. Francis Biddle, Attorney General of the United States; Irving Olds of U. S.

Steel; Alger Hiss; Augustin Derby of the law faculty of New York University. They told me about Holmes's methods of work, the turns and surprises of his mind in action. They talked of his courtesy and courtly manners, told how the house in Washington overflowed with young people who came any time, dropping in as late as midnight, and always welcome. "Holmes was skeptical of everything save life itself," said Biddle. The secretaries had loved the Judge, they wanted to tell me stories forever. They had all the time in the world, they protested, following me to the door. It's good to talk about the old man, they said; it brings him back.

In Boston there had been gossip and joking about the Judge's predilection for burlesque shows. The men who told me seemed pleased; they liked to think of this remote, ironic creature as displaying what they called a human trait. But I had been wary. Even if the stories were true, a printed page has far more impact than the jovial talk of friends, and I had wondered how best to handle the matter. The picture of an aging Judge, sitting with the bald heads in the second row, was somehow hard to compass and would be hard to tell without distortion.

Tom Corcoran was explicit on the point. "No!" he said, and slapped the hotel lunch table with the flat of his hand. "Holmes never went near a burlycue. I would know it, nobody could call me a finicking character. If Holmes talked about it, it was because he wanted to be one of the boys. He was a true intellectual, he lived on his high hill and he got lonely. He had to make them think he was one of the boys, one of the fellows. I will bet you fifty dollars," Corcoran said, "a hundred dollars, you can't prove Holmes ever sat in a burlesque show, anyway not after he was forty and a judge."

I believed Tom Corcoran and I left out the burlesque shows, though when my book appeared I received angry letters, demanding if I were a prude, or if I thought the Judge a prude. Of the twelve law secretaries interviewed, only one refused to talk. This man had been with Holmes when he died. He did not approve of my writing the book and said so, said also that he preferred not to talk to me of Holmes's death. I rose at once to take my leave, but as I reached the door he called me back. "On the whole," he said, "it may do less harm to tell you than not to tell you. I will write you what you have asked, and what you want to know."

I never heard from him. By a rare stroke of luck, however, I learned of a Holmes niece who had often visited the family in Washington. Dorothy Vaughan, she was; Mrs. Wayland Vaughan, wife of the oceanographer. Holmes's old coachman, Charles Buckley, told me about her when he drove me to Arlington to show me Holmes's grave. I called on Mrs. Vaughan and spent a night at her house in Georgetown. We talked about the Judge all evening, and as I left next day she handed me a battered cardboard box, tied with red tape. "Here are some letters," she said. "Just go through them and see if there is anything you can use, then send them back." On the train to Philadelphia I opened the box and the letters. One was from a Boston relative, a man I had met and talked with, who had been present when Holmes died in Washington. He had written back to Boston, much moved with what he had seen.

I thought of Mr. Palfrey, to whom I had made no

promise aside from the unpublished letters that he had shown me. I said a prayer and rejoiced at what fate had put into my hands. Later, I returned to Washington and talked with the Marshal of the Supreme Court, with pages who had served Justice Holmes — with anyone, indeed, who could describe the routine of the household at 1720 Eye Street. James Doherty, Courthouse Messenger in Boston, told me how he came to Washington with Holmes by train on the Friday of first arrival, December 2, 1902, and what ensued on that memorable day, in the middle of a coal strike. The house at Eye Street stone-cold, the dealers wanting to know if this judge was to be a regular customer, and asking who the devil was Oliver Wendell Holmes. . . . Doherty, like Tom Corcoran, possessed the Irish sense of scene. Arthur Thomas, the tall old Negro who had been messenger so long in the Supreme Court, told me, "I've served many gentlemen, but never one like him. I was powerful fond of Judge Holmes, and I think he liked me, too."

These men showed no surprise when I asked for small detail, Holmes's daily habits, the exact spot where certain furniture was placed in the Eye Street house, which was the Judge's favorite chair and whether various windows faced south or west. From a Washington photographer I bought nine views of the interior of the house, clear and telling — pictures of Holmes's library, the desk where he worked, of the dining room and of Holmes's bedroom with the white iron bedstead. Dorothy Vaughan described the furniture, gave me the provenance of certain family silver, told me which pieces came from whence. Again, I was dealing in minutiae. Yet of what else is portraiture constructed? If an actor on the stage planned to play Justice Holmes, would he scorn to know the way Holmes held his hands when he sat down, or if the old man smacked his lips while eating?

Even if I should not use these things, I would have them by me, I would know them and they would help me to see my characters. With Mrs. Holmes in particular, such detail was essential. A woman's life is built largely of tangible matters; the furniture of her house is part of the furniture of her spirit. I was surprised when I learned from Dorothy Vaughan that Mrs. Holmes had a white fur rug beside her bed; I had thought of Fanny Dixwell as too austere for such. Garden Street, Cambridge, where she was bred, had not, I felt sure, gone in for white fur bedroom rugs. I was pleased when I thought of it; Mrs. Holmes must have enjoyed that rug.

My own philosophy of biography is by no means a physical, material one. It was Holmes's mind and character that I had ambition to depict — his life as a whole, its effect on others and on the nation at large. "The ferment of genius is quickly imparted," Holmes had said. "When a man is great he makes others believe in greatness." I planned to quote his words at length — speeches, dissents, legal opinions. Readers will not suffer many lines set off in small print, or too many lofty intellectual quotations, unless these are placed in scene; I had learned it long ago. Let the reader see Holmes as he spoke, hear the timbre of his voice, glance at the room where he stood and know the occasion. The so-called "intellectual man" cannot be portrayed without scene; indeed, I think it presumptuous to try. I have heard it said that the aim of Holmes's biography should be to "place him in the stream of American intellectual consciousness." I am suspicious of such a statement. It is too high-toned, it savors of gobbledygook. I am by no means sure there is such a "stream," such a historical entity — and if there is, that Holmes can be "placed" in it. To me, the elusiveness of Holmes's position is one of the most characteristic things about him.

I was nearing the end of my search; the time approached when I must stop seeking and begin to write. Toward the end, I had an interview which I thought at the time was a failure but which later proved to be one of the most fruitful I had undertaken. The man interviewed was one of Holmes's law secretaries, who at the moment held high position in our wartime government. In Boston he had been described to me as "dry and intellectual"; I had been warned that he was not a man who "gave out."

The interview took place in a Washington hotel, at lunch. Because this man had little time to waste, I did not stop to explain that the writing of biography is primarily a matter of reducing the large scenes to a series of small pictures that can be encompassed by the naked eye. Instead, I pulled from my purse a notebook and list of queries, and began.

The gentleman listened, ate his lunch, made one or two replies. "When Justice Holmes, at eighty-seven, had been sitting and stood up, did he," I asked, "have trouble gaining balance? Did he totter?"

The lawyer set down his coffee cup. His voice was cold. "The trivia for which you are searching," he said, "I long ago discarded in favor of a larger, rounded picture of the Judge."

It was my fault and I knew it. I should have explained. I did not, that day, recover this lawyer's confidence. Nevertheless he bore with me, answered my questions, and what he said revealed much of Holmes's extraordinary way of meeting life in his old age. This secretary had been with the Judge when Mrs. Holmes died, in 1928, and had seen Justice Holmes, in the midst of grief, write his magnificent dissent in *United States versus Rosika Schwimmer.* . . . *"If there is any principle of the Constitution that more imperatively calls for attachment than any other it is the principle of free thought — not free thought for those who agree with us but freedom for the thought that we hate."*

"I saw philosophy tested in a hard hour," the lawyer said. "Holmes had always believed that life was action, the use of one's powers. His wife died, and Holmes's routine never broke. He just kept on and did his work. He was living out his philosophy."

I thanked the lawyer and took my leave. Three years later, when my book appeared, I had a long, cordial letter from him. The lawyer said he liked what I had written, and it surprised him. Did I recall our luncheon, and had I noticed, that day, how he was cautious in what he said? He was sorry, now, that he had not talked more freely.

I went straight from that lunch table to interview Justice Brandeis. At eighty-seven, one year of life remained to him. His apartment was bleak, entirely undistinguished, bare of the usual accumulations of living — signed photographs, knickknacks, the small comforts of old age. It had a look of transience, impersonality. The old man sat at a desk with his back to the window; light shone through his fluffy white hair. He wore no glasses, his hearing was perfect. The face was bony, strongly outlined, and this leanness extended to his body, giving a noticeable effect of youth. He spoke quietly, slowly, there was an austerity about him. It was the only time in my life that I have had the feeling I was talking with a saint — a saint moreover with a quick, remarkable intelligence that made itself manifest before he spoke.

Brandeis showed no impatience when I asked for detail. "But of course, take notes," he said, in answer to my question. "Certainly! You might forget, or make a mistake of fact."

Justice Brandeis was the one person left who had been in the Boston offices of Shattuck and Monroe in the 1870's, when Holmes worked there as a lawyer. Could he describe the rooms? I asked. When you walked in the door, what lay to the right and the left, and where did Holmes have his desk?

Brandeis was quiet for a minute. "Holmes sat in the back office, to the right," he said. "You had to walk through Shattuck's office to get there. Magnitsky sat in the entrance, at a table. He was a sort of greeter, an office helper. Captain Magnitsky. He had been in the war with Holmes, in Holmes's regiment."

But of course — I knew Magnitsky. He had served with young Captain Holmes in the Twentieth Regiment, Massachusetts Volunteers, and then had fallen on evil days; Holmes had rescued him. Justice Brandeis finished a careful description and broke off. "Holmes was a great man," he said. "A great man. Never let anyone persuade you otherwise. Before I came on the bench, I practiced law for thirty-eight years. I sweated it out. I had to, earning my living. That's how I learned. Holmes didn't have to. He was raised in his father's library. He was aloof, he had an ivory tower quality. But he *knew*. He knew by profound insight. It's good to have an ivory tower man on the bench, once in a generation."

Lawyers are inclined to exactness; they do not like fuzzy

questions. But I risked it; I did not think this man would be caustic or clever at my expense. "People like to call Holmes a skeptic," I said. "Some call him heartless. Mr. Justice, did you ever hear Holmes express a conviction about mankind, a philosophic conviction?"

Brandeis thought a minute. "Holmes had a conviction that man should be free in a large way. He was a great liberator. He was a great emancipator."

I stood up to say good-by. Brandeis smiled and walked with me to the door. "Holmes was always kind to the lawyers who argued with us," he said.

I took a cab to the Union Station, and before boarding my train, sat in the waiting room to write up my notes. (What Brandeis said remained of course unchanged; my notes concerned the man himself, and my impressions of him.) Brandeis had had an extraordinary effect upon me. I scribbled over about ten pages of a small pocket notebook, and at the end I quoted something which had little bearing on facts, interviews or the nervous planning of biographical chapters: *"I hear no good news ever, save some trait of noble character."*

The words I think are Thoreau's. Eighteen years have passed, since that day, but as I look at the notebook the spell is still upon me. "Great men confess old age," I had scrawled in the margin, sideways. "They accept old age, and thereby deepen the narrowing channel that remains open to them."

It reads a trifle sententiously, as ideas are apt to on first writing. Yet it is true, and Brandeis taught it to me. Brandeis . . . Bishop Lawrence in Boston, pink-faced and shrewd . . . President Lowell, very deaf and very witty . . . Miss Loring of Pride's Crossing, ninety-three and stone-blind . . . The old Negro, Arthur Thomas, who drove Holmes's carriage and who, each year after Holmes's death, sent the Washington *Star* a little piece he wrote about the Justice. "My Tributes," Thomas called them, and the paper printed them.

Here in Washington I was drawing closer to the old Holmes, the "magnificent old man," and now I did not resent his age but welcomed it. Chief Justice Stone, when I interviewed him, was a mere seventy — he had come to the Supreme Court in 1925. But what he said pertained to the theme: "Holmes grew, after eighty, grew in legal stature."

In my penciled notes the words are underlined. Stone told me a little story about Holmes, at ninety. Yehudi Menuhin, then a child prodigy, played the violin in Washington. Stone heard him, and next morning told Holmes about it. Amazing, Stone said, to see this ordinary, healthy boy come out and put his bow to the strings — and suddenly there was magic. Holmes cared little for music but he admired first-rate performance in any field. He wished he could do something like that, he said, to which Stone replied, "A lot of us wish we could write opinions like yours." Holmes, pleased, told Stone he did pretty well himself along those lines, and Stone murmured a conventional denial. "My boy," Holmes said with gusto, "you needn't think you can fool God by *that* deprecating remark."

The wit of old age has a matchless quality, when it comes — a hard-bitten saltiness that penetrates without hurt. As an old man, Holmes's glance was piercing; people often spoke of it. Doctors said there was no *arcus senilis,* or gray rim around the cornea. "Holmes wasn't easy on people," one of his law secretaries had told me. "That glance could terrify." And so it should, I thought; old men ought to be terrible. They carry about them an Old Testament flavor. Was not Moses terrible, and Noah, whose sons obeyed his voice?

Chief Justice Hughes, when I saw him, also testified to Holmes's mental growth in old age. When Holmes came to the Court in 1902, he wrote lengthy opinions. "Too long," Hughes said, "like the one on Northern Securities. By the time I got there (1910) he was writing shorter opinions. More literary. But make no mistake," Hughes added, "Holmes was mature when he came."

The word brought me up short. Mature, at sixty-one? It occurred to me that some people are not grown up at sixty or at ninety-six; genuine maturity is a noteworthy achievement. Chief Justice Hughes, when I interviewed him, was just turned eighty-one. In answer to my letter he had invited me to his house in Washington. It was late afternoon when I was ushered into a drawing room big enough for Buckingham Palace. At the far end of it, by a window, stood Justice and Mrs. Hughes, white-haired, slight, erect and silent. I began the journey across that shining floor and in my eagerness I all but ran. I saw the two smile; by the time I reached them we were all three smiling, though nobody had said a word.

For nearly two hours, Justice Hughes talked; Mrs. Hughes gave us tea from a little table set before her. "Holmes never spoke to me of his father," Hughes said. "But he liked to talk about his Uncle John Holmes."

I nodded. "Uncle John was the good-natured one," I put in. "The one with no ambition, whom everyone loved. Uncle John liked birds, and he liked to sit on Cambridge Common in the sun, near his house."

"Yes," Hughes said. "Uncle John used to tell Wendell,

'You must be vulgar, Wendell. Don't forget to be vulgar.' "
At eighty-odd, Justice Holmes was interested not only in the
cases as they came up, Hughes went on, but in the lawyers,
"the whole thing." He could write a summary of a case while
the lawyer was talking. "A very hard thing to do," Hughes
added. "After lunch, when the judges came back to the bench,
Holmes used to put his fingers to his forehead and take a nap
— but not until he had the case straight in his mind." One
time, Hughes poked him. Holmes sat up. "Jesus Christ!" he
said. Hughes, telling the story, repeated the oath in full voice.
It was wonderful to hear him, sitting there, himself possessed
of the dignity, courage and distinction of his own great
career.

Once more I was glad that I was writing about an old
man, and that magnificent old men had shown me the model,
as it were. I thought of the things that Holmes himself had
said, as he saw old age approaching. At fifty-eight: "We
gray-haired men hear in our ears the roar of the cataract, and
know that we are very near." At ninety, in the famous radio
birthday speech: "Riders in a race do not stop short of the goal.
Death plucks my ears and says, Live! I am coming." Best of
all were the words that Holmes wrote, at eighty-three, to a
young Chinese law student in Washington, named Wu: "If
I were dying my last words would be, *Have faith and pursue
the unknown end.*"

No young person could have said that. I knew it, now;
a biographer can learn obliquely. And the evidence of a man's
life needs corroboration. All of these people had taught me
about Judges Holmes — the ladies, the courthouse janitors,
the law secretaries, the Bishop of Massachusetts, the three
Justices of the United States Supreme Court. And they had

taught me, not only by what they remembered of Judge Holmes, but by what they were themselves. Sometimes I had been impatient, I had thought the personalities of those bright talkers got in the way of the past and of the picture I was seeking. I had wanted to turn the conversation away from themselves and back to Holmes.

But I had been wrong. A man's memory is part of himself, it cannot be taken out of context. An interviewer, I have sometimes thought, is like a woman invited to waltz to music; she must follow easily, no matter how intricate the side steps. A little tactful steering can put the conversation back on track, but there is no room for forcing or impatience.

My research was not complete; research is never completed, even when one's book is ended and has gone to the printer. Around the corner lurks another possibility of interview, another book to read, a courthouse to explore, a document to verify.

Yet Holmes, the young man and the old, had begun to take shape, emerge, protest his quality. Interviews, letters, scenes from printed volumes, the remembered sound of voices, the rooms where one heard testimony and took down evidence — there was a fusing, a sense of continuity. I could not recreate a man. But with the material I had gathered I should be able to suggest him, perhaps evoke him, with his living quality.

5
The Company of Scholars

It is the finest company in the world
— bright, quick-thinking, slow-talking, maddening, invigorat-
ing, challenging. Dr. Johnson once said that writers should
converse, when possible, with lawyers; "lawyers know life
practically, they have what the writer wants." It is true, yet
true also that the biographer — this biographer, certainly —
needs the company of scholars, teachers of history, writers of
learned monographs, directors of seminars. These scholars
have chosen, each one, a period, a topic, a "field," within the
confines of which he will live and operate for a lifetime.
No specialist is glib or facile with his facts. And this very care
sets the biographer free, lets him leap the centuries with his
speculations and his queries.

The professor is deliberate, he dislikes snap judgment,
clever retorts at the expense of sincerity. Besides, he does not
want to be caught wrong in his premises. There is a primal
delightful innocence in him; he tells a funny story with all
the gusto of Adam telling it for the first time to Eve. And

he is tough-fibered in his profession: a scorching review of his latest book is published in the historical quarterly, and next Christmas holiday the author sits with the reviewer at the historians' convention, companionably drinking beer in the hotel bar. The professors laugh at themselves, they laugh at life; they long ago abjured the bitch-goddess Success, and the best of them will fight for his scholastic ideals with a courage and persistence that would shame a soldier. The professor is not afraid of words like *truth;* in fact he is not afraid of words at all. Like the lawyer he loves to talk and teach, loves to exercise his mind and knows he does it well. But unlike the lawyer, the professor has a wonderful confidence, somehow, that there is time to talk.

If today I seek the scholar's company from inclination, at the outset I sought it from direst need. *Yankee from Olympus* was scarcely delivered to the publisher when I began study for a life of John Adams, second President of the United States. This first of the New England clan, this "Honest John, Old Sink or Swim," was as different from O. W. Holmes, Jr., as a man can be. John Adams was plain-born, his father a farmer and deacon of the church in Braintree, Massachusetts, population 1500. Here was no plot of a man born at the top and holding his position. Here was no ivory-tower intellectual but a creature of earth and appetite, who carried about him always a provincial, solid, small-town quality. "Not graceful," Jefferson said of him, "not elegant, not always fluent in his public addresses, he yet came out with a power both of thought and expression, which moved us from our seats. To John Adams more than to any other man is the country indebted for its independence."

How was I going to find this person, this human being

who lived two hundred years ago? If the guild of legal scholars had buried Justice Holmes in laurels, the schoolbooks had buried John Adams in pious, Founding Fathers eulogy. My friends of liberal politics put him down as a hopeless conservative, a stuffy old Federalist. I read Adams's diary, begun when he was twenty-one, I read his correspondence with his wife Abigail and caught no echo of conservatism. "I have a Zeal at heart," wrote the young Adams, "for my Country and her friends, which I cannot smother or conceal; it will burn out at times and in companies where it ought to be latent in my breast. Colonel Otis' phrase is, 'The zeal-pot boils over.'"

Benjamin Franklin, in Paris with Adams in the 1780's, said that Adams was capable of going suddenly quite crazy, steaming off half-cocked and making all kinds of trouble in diplomatic relations. Adams knew it and used to caution himself. *"Sobrius esto, John,* be not carried away by sudden blasts of wind, by unexpected flashes of lightning." Odd, that such a man should throw his heart into matters so abstract as government. Yet John Adams had a talent for government, a kind of artistic obsession with it. Early in life he studied the republics of the world and compared them. When his friends would not correspond with him on the subject, he complained. "I know not how it is, but mankind have an aversion to the science of government. Is it because the subject is too dry? To me, no romance is more entertaining."

To write about John Adams, I must know something of comparative government. Above all, I must know about colonial America. As a boy, as a student at Harvard College and as a young lawyer, John Adams had been proud of being an Englishman. I must study this old loyalty, know how men and women felt during the long slow dangerous approach of independence and the federal idea. Adams, early and late, wrote about governments and constitutions with the fervor of a lover writing to his mistress. Here, in short, was that rare bird, a patriot, the first I had met that I could believe in wholly. John Adams must be described as a man set and molded in colonial America, British America, where men who had never seen England spoke of London as "home," and where Bostonians felt themselves nearer to Europe than to North Carolina.

It was a broader task than I had hitherto undertaken. I was ignorant of the place, the scene, the time. Small wonder that I sought out the professors, asking questions that had no answers. . . . What, actually was the function of government? And what did Adams mean when he spoke of law in such reverent and loving terms? — "That most excellent monument of human art, the common law of England."

The common law: how did one find out about *that?* Dictionary definitions were not enough, and my questions had no end. Is a unicameral assembly necessarily radical, like the Pennsylvania Assembly in 1776? How much space should I give to the Seven Years War, and what if England had accepted Guadeloupe instead of Canada at the peace table? Was it true that, but for Britain, the American colonies might have become a mere strip of French holdings along the Atlantic coast? Reading Lawrence Gipson on *The Great War for the Empire,* my mind had turned a somersault. Were the history books wrong, then, and had our war for independence been a grave mistake, a tragic, stupid, unnecessary error? There must be a way, short of a lifetime, to find out which history books were true and which were false. The question seemed naive, I hesitated to ask it. But when I finally dared it the professors did not laugh but shook their heads gravely and said that was the very question by which their lives were ruled and upon which their days were spent.

My previous biographies had not led me into this company of scholars; my companions along the way had been musicians, lawyers, judges. Justice Holmes moreover could be counted almost as contemporary. Even though he fought at Antietam, he did not die until 1935, and the Civil War was still within living memories. My own mother had once remarked, in general conversation, that as a child in West Philadelphia she had been kept indoors, one fine hot July day, "because of the soldiers, straggling back from the battle." When I inquired, "What battle?" my mother replied, a little cross at my stupidity, "Why, the battle of Gettysburg, of course."

Tschaikovsky, even the brothers Rubinstein had made their music in times comparatively recent. But with John Adams I had jumped two centuries. I could no longer rely on an overlapping of the generations, a bringing of news direct to now. The techniques of research must replace the techniques of interviewing; everything must be found in book or artifact, noted down, verified and collated. Words like collated had hitherto been foreign to me; I began to use them and to step cautiously in the forest of historical bibliography. One morning, near the beginning of my work, I went to the Haverford College Library and planted myself before the shelves of eighteenth-century American history. I had stood there perhaps an hour, taking volumes down and putting them back, when I heard a jovial voice behind me. It was Professor Drake, of the History Department. "What are you doing *here,* Mrs. Bowen?" he said. "This isn't your century! Don't tell me you are jumping the fence a hundred years and writing about the Federal era?"

I felt like a poacher, hunting without a permit. And I had chosen, it was clear, a period appallingly rich in documentation. To write about John Adams needed three hands for taking notes, two sets of eyes for reading, days forty-eight hours long. No period has been more thoroughly explored; historians have poked and peered through every crack and crevice. I saw that lack of space might force me to leave out great important chunks and portions . . . the triangular trade from Britain to New England to the West Indies . . . British home politics, the very significant attitudes of her ministers, Grenville, Bute, Pitt, Camden, Newcastle, Rockingham. I wrote whole chapters about these men, not excluding George III, whose letters had astonished me. Then I threw my chapters in the wastebasket, groaning as I did it and saying prayers of apology to scholars like Namier, Van Tyne and Nevins.

In my workbook I complained of being overwhelmed by the vast quantity of my notes, just as in writing Tchaikovsky I had been overwhelmed by his letters, until my own pages sounded as if Tchaikovsky had written them in his sleep. According to the workbook I was also beset by Indians. "During the 1750's and 60's it was Indians that occupied us," I noted. "Massachusetts was always talking about sending ambassadors to the Six Nations to make a separate peace. Yet from my chapters so far, one would think the Indians never existed except those Ponkhapoags that came to the Adams's back door."

Should I ask the professors what to do about Indians?

And which professors? The ones near home, at Bryn Mawr College, Haverford College and the University of Pennsylvania, were occupied with other matters, each in his field of economics, comparative religion, or problems of land tenure and the frontier. I argued with myself, on paper. "Never mind about Indians and Guadeloupe. I can't take the cosmic over-all view." I was not up in an airplane, I was walking on earth with John Adams. Codfish and Protestantism — that's what John Adams's Massachusetts was interested in.

Perhaps I was taking too many notes, anesthetizing myself in the pleasures of reading and research? I recalled a pair of young scholars I had met in Worcester, Massachusetts, while reading in the American Antiquarian Society. "How we dread the time," one of them had said, "when we finish research and have to write our books!" It is an occupational disease of scholars, this eternal taking of notes; some historians, like Lord Acton, never get their books written at all. There are so many procedures, so many precious cherished techniques of manipulating those neat blank cards, five inches by eight. Book title, author, date and place of publication, pages cited must be written in the upper left-hand corner, neatly pinned down for reference. If one does not pin it all down, if one omits a single item of identification, chaos can ensue.

Yet there is danger in overmeticulousness, concerning the mechanics of research. For myself, if I am too elaborate in libraries I lose the thread of what I am hunting. The over-all picture fades, the pace slows, the heart goes out of me and the story that had been so bright shrivels to a neat dead pile of notes, cards and "documentation." Better to chance it, neglect an item in that sacred left-hand corner and spend a

dreary day in verifying, later on, when one's manuscript has
been delivered to the printer. In the third year of my work
on John Adams I argued this point with a history professor.
He seemed startled, and after a brief silence suggested that
I attend the historians' conference next month — the big convention that meets annually in the Christmas holidays. This
winter it was to be in an eastern city. I could meet all the
professors; some, whose books I admired would surely be
there. The Schlesingers, Senior and Junior; Wertenbaker,
Dumas Malone, Roy Nichols, Commager, Nevins, John Miller
who wrote *Origins of the American Revolution*.

It was a dazzling thought. I protested, however, that I
did not belong at a professors' convention; I would feel shy.
And how could a person like me get in? Would there be
other writers present — professional writers, as opposed to
professional scholars?

Five dollars annual dues, prepaid, would get me in, the
professor replied succinctly. And what did I mean, "as
opposed to"? If there was opposition, there shouldn't be.
(I think he used the word *dichotomy*.) "Come along!" the
professor said, vigorously. "Speak your mind and see what
happens. You will learn something. And so," he added, much
to my gratification, "so perhaps will we."

In the Grand Ballroom we sat in rows, on folding chairs
of aluminum. At 10 A.M. the hotel chandeliers gave out their
morning light, hard and a trifle tired. Whole blocks of
seats were vacant, the plastic cushions shone. Yet I had never
seen so many professors at one place in my life. Hundreds
of them, and hundreds more in the hotel corridors, roaming
from Section to Section, stopping in at Parlor B for "Social

Responsibility and the Medieval Mystics," at Parlor C for "Uniformities in History," at the Garden Room for something about pragmatic history and the challenge of teaching in the professional schools. There were professors from California, Texas, Florida, New York; young instructors and grizzled handsome old department heads in tweed coats and gray flannel trousers. There were nuns from the Catholic colleges, whispering down the passages in pairs, black gowns floating, spectacles gleaming.

In front of me the chairman rose, introducing a panel of professors who were to talk on "Aristocracy in the Politics of Colonial Virginia." I got out my notebook and pencil; looking about me I saw that nobody else was taking notes. I had joined, as it were, a new club, and the charter members surprised me. In their persons they were other than I had thought. Professor Schlesinger looked like a bank president, I would have trusted him with my last cent. The great Professor McIlwain of Harvard might have been senior board member of a North Shore Hunt Club, distinguished and easy in his tweeds.

Not only their persons surprised me, but their point of view. The dichotomy before mentioned was very plain; it was indeed present and blooming each minute of the day, in public discussion and in private, at the lunch table and the hotel cocktail bar. I must practice, I thought, a quicker recoil. Sitting in their conferences, a biographer had need of toughness. From their platforms the scholars were forever taking shots at biography. "The dangers of the biographical approach," they said. I knew what they meant, of course. Biography is written from a point of view; the writer likes his hero or dislikes him. Moreover, biography is filled with personal detail, those "particulars" to which the historian does not "descend" without apology. To the professional historian, biography has for centuries been tainted. Laurence Echard, writing his preface to Volume II of a *History of England* (published in 1718), said that he had "several times deviated and descended from the Dignity of an Historian, and voluntarily fallen into the lower class of Biographers, Annalists, &c." Sir Walter Ralegh, being a poet, was braver. In Book IV of his *History of the World* — written from his prison cell in the Tower — Ralegh made a nice little statement of explanation. "I think it is not impertinent sometimes to relate such accidents as may seem no better than mere trifles; for even by trifles are the qualities of great Persons as well disclosed as by their great actions."

I thought of it, sitting in the Grand Ballroom or roaming the mezzanine to look at the publishers' exhibitions — college textbooks, reference books, manuals on the preparation of Ph.D. theses. The ancients, I remembered, were free of any snobbism concerning the "biographical approach." Herodotus, Thucydides, Tacitus, Livy described whom and what they would and let us know exactly what they thought. My own search for detail was frank and purposeful. Yet I knew that I had wasted hours and days in misplaced historical enthusiasms, later discarded; I was apt to follow false trails. These learned professors, these fortunate possessors of Ph.D.'s, must surely have developed a fool-proof procedure. Somewhere up their academic sleeves they had a *méthode,* a *système,* as the vocal department had called it in my music school days. From these scholars I could learn short-cuts, more efficient ways of finding what I wanted to know.

The trouble was that what the professors wanted to

know and what I wanted to know were turning out to be so different. Or perhaps our variance lay rather in the uses to which we put our knowledge. Variance? It was a professor's word; a bottomless chasm divided us. I was slow to see it, much slower than the professors were. There had been an occasion, some time before the convention, that should have told me. At home in Philadelphia I had met a history professor, a man in his early forties, who like me was writing a life of John Adams. It was his sabbatical year, the professor said, and he was traveling from library to library all over the United States, looking for holographs and manuscripts — letters and documents signed by John Adams. At once I had been filled with interest and at the same time, alarm. (Whose book would reach the public first?) Yet it was good to find somebody I could talk to, someone who cared about John Adams and would know the names and places, the scenes and persons and eighteenth-century states of mind with which I had become familiar. Together we had left the research library where we were working and crossed the street at noon for lunch. It happened that I had lately returned from one of my pilgrimages to the Adams houses in Braintree, near Boston — the clapboard cottage where John Adams was born and the house next door into which he moved when he married his enchanting Abigail.

As usual, following one of these visits, I was excited and wanted to talk. "What luck," I told the professor, "what extraordinary, unequaled luck for us biographers, that those Adams houses still stand!" Had the professor seen John Adams's beaver hat and the red wool cloak he wore, riding circuit? Fire-engine red, it was, and must have covered him to the boots. And the attic room that John slept in as a boy, with the hired man's room behind it — that was a sight for biographers! Sitting on John's bed I could touch the ceiling with my hand. From the front door downstairs to the stone wall by the road was only fifteen steps; I had paced it off. "Professor," I said, "do you think the old Plymouth Road ran that close to the house in, say, 1745, when John Adams was ten years old?"

The professor shook his head. "Haven't seen those houses," he said. "Don't intend to. I never go to Boston, I hate the place."

He was like Sir Edward Coke, I had thought: *Non lego non credo*. Was this professor an exception, or was the academic mind deliberately trained to distrust the evidence of the senses? Your artist, when it comes to the pinch, trusts little else. Surely, it takes all five senses to apprehend mankind, past or present? History was not made by ghosts and should not be told as if ghosts made it. Ghosts did not sit in the Continental Congress, write the Declaration of Independence and fight a war with England. A ghost did not build Mount Vernon, with its green terraces above the Potomac. Integrity is in the lines of that house, culture is in it. God knows where a Virginia farmer got his culture, or a Braintree Adams his vision of government. That they got it is one of America's miracles.

In the Chicago Historical Society I had seen two suits of John Adams's clothes, stuffed out on forms, and at the Braintree cottage his wedding vest of white satin, embroidered by his mother in sprigs of golden wheat, to bring luck to a farmer. But at the historians' convention I did not mention these things; I had learned better and besides, I had come here not to talk but to listen. Nevertheless I was reminded of the professor who had hated Boston; in parlors and on panels I met his double. At the supper table, one of these young men inquired how many copies of *Yankee from Olympus* had been sold, to date. When I told him, he whistled. "Some day," he said, "I'm going to take a year off and write a popular book."

The sheer arrogance of it silenced me; upon such a young man, retort would be wasted. But I thought of him often, that day and the next. Could it be that the cold hand of the Herr Doktor von Ranke lay even yet upon the campus, and must the onus of writing a popular book be so hard to bear? Yet books that are well written seem doomed to popularity; the public is avid for history. And the professors spend a good third of their time in writing; most universities require publication from the faculty. Their books are distinguished, a powerful, indispensable contribution. Without these learned volumes and monographs and all this hard work of digging among the sources, no biographer could proceed at all.

But the longer I stayed at the convention, the more I wondered how the professors managed it. I thought of the manual on the mezzanine, "How to Write a Ph.D. Thesis." By diagram and example it listed what the student must not do — directions so complicated they hardly read like English. After such a dose, I, for one, would not be able to write the alphabet, let alone teach it. Had it become mere ritual, then, this graduate scholarship that I had thought I envied? Was it only a magic brew, to be swallowed with appropriate incantations, and must a person's whole life be spent afterwards recovering? I could not believe it. These scholars knew better than I the criterion for a good history book. Surely, they did not wish it to be dry and to stop at mere correctness, authenticity of fact and a reasonable continuity of narrative? Yet as a writer I was troubled by certain attitudes and aspects of the younger scholars. It was as if some dragon had roared at them, some Medusa had shaken her gory locks, and at a time of life when these heroes should be pursuing the Golden Fleece, they steered their barks toward safety. It was none of my business, but I spoke of it to one of the professors, a man I knew well, and he responded with feeling. He said there was indeed danger for historians in the Ph.D. training — he called it "the Ph.D. octopus." With a lively shuffling of metaphor he said the Ph.D. octopus was running amok, trampling the vineyard to dust, at the same time training the young mind and sucking the young heart dry. It was a touchy subject to bring up in conference, the professor added — too many toes got stepped on. What would I think of a meeting next semester, just a small one, to discuss ways of getting art into history?

That would be an even more touchy subject, I thought. And I recalled an incident of some years ago, when I had gone for help to a most distinguished historian. Two chapters of a biography that I was working on would not come round; a scene which by historical right should be thrilling lay flat on my pages and dead, though I had tried writing it half a dozen ways. . . . Had I plenty of data, well authenticated? the professor asked. When I said yes, first-rate material and more than I could use, the professor shrugged and inquired what I was worried about. "Go home," he said, "and write it from your cards."

Write it from my cards. This scholar, who himself had published books of history, and who knew so much that I could never know — was he suggesting that I set up those five-by-eight cards on the desk and deliberately transpose them from A to Z? Did he mean I should forget historical "plot" and story, forget the reader, too, and the hard exciting fact that written history is communication? Communication! a delicate, desperate business to undertake on the high level of history....

The incident had gone from my mind. But here at the historians' convention it came back with force. Was this, then, the thing that divided me from the professors, these men and women whose work was so like my own yet so unlike? I had come to the conference to learn; I had thought to sit in reverent silence. Yet I found myself wanting to shout and argue. These scholars forced my mind to grapple with the problem at hand, to define terms and literary ideals, my reasons for writing about Holmes and John Adams. *What is this book about and why am I impelled to write it?* These are the hardest questions the biographer has to face.

Something, in this place of scholars, had touched the vital center of my work, and concerned not only the approach to biography but the writing of it.

6
Scholars and Challengers

Sir Edward Coke's grandson, Roger Coke, compiled, in the seventeenth century, a wild and useful history of his times, entitled *A Detection of the Court and State of England*. In it he damned all Royalists and praised all Parliament men. "I expect," said his preface, "it will be objected against me, that in writing this History, I have sometimes been transported into an Heat unbecoming an Historian: I answer, that it may happen a Man may be angry, and not sin." The best part of the *Detection* is its fury; by it one is transported back in time; one feels the danger and the fear, a country torn in two, awaiting the coming of that dark Puritan Oliver who was to lead rebellion.

Bias, point of view, fury — are they then so dangerous and must they be ironed out of history, the hills flattened and the contours leveled? The professors talked about passion and point of view in history as a Calvinist talks about sin in the bedroom. There they sat, trying to get the heat out of history and here I sat, trying to get it in. There must surely be a balance between us somewhere, a place for us to meet. . . .

Perhaps it all depended on what one asked of history, what one looked for in reading it. A point of view and a special lighting are not distortions, says Santayana. "They are conditions of vision, and spirit can see nothing not focused in some living eye." For the biographer, one of the hardest things is to *find* his bias, find the platform upon which he stands, accept and recognize his reason for writing this especial book. Montesquieu, in his foreword to *The Spirit of Laws,* explains that at the outset of work he had great trouble in expressing himself, and even in recalling and utilizing what he had read upon the subject. Ideas eluded him, and even as he touched upon them they slipped and were gone. "But when I once discovered my first principles, everything I sought for appeared, and . . . I have seen my work begin, growing up, advancing to maturity, and finished."

Old John Strype celebrated his ninetieth birthday in the year 1734. Writing his annals of the Reformation, Strype told a story and then added, "This was not fair, to say no worse. But I must remember that I am not now writing an Apology but an History: And therefore I forbear to add anything more on this subject." Modern writing does not permit these little asides to the reader; I have often thought it a pity. Why should not the author say outright what he thinks and let us know that it is not history but opinion? "When they publish sketches of their finds," wrote Jusserand, "paleontologists show by a plain line what the earth has yielded, and by a dotted one what, according to their speculations, the rest would have been like. The historian must do the same, that the reader may know what is certain and what is only probable."

John Adams himself, when he was old, had ideas on the

subject. "I have very solemn notions of the sanctity of history," he wrote. "I pretend to nothing more than to furnish memorials to serve historians. It is their duty to detect my errors and appreciate every Thing according to its true value. I doubt whether faithful history ever was or ever can be written."

No historian worth his salt but has felt the same doubt. Professor Whitehead once declared "pure" history to be impossible, the notion a "figment of the imagination. The historian in his description of the past depends on his own judgment as to what constitutes the importance of human life."

The importance of human life and what constitutes it: not an easy question to answer or even to ask. Here in convention assembled the professors chose to pass it by. And in truth the asking of it spelled danger, though it so happens the biographer must ask it on every page. Biased history is of course the worst of sins. What I asked for, what I missed in academic history was not a bias toward events or nations but a point of view toward life, some hint that the writer belonged to the human race and had himself experienced passion, grief or disappointment. In this conference hotel, among these Sections and Parlors and Divisions, perhaps I had missed direction. Was it the philosophers I should be following? The importance of human life is, in truth, a bit cosmic for technical discussion, for precise thinking a trifle fuzzy round the edges.

Yet the concept was no more difficult than the phrases used to blanket it. I had heard some very fancy words concerning relative objectivity in historiography. I heard also about skeptical relativism, technocratic rationalism, determinism,

positivism, and presentism. The first time I heard the word
presentism I went out and looked it up in three dictionaries.
It was not there. Next day the professors themselves defined
it. Should the historian, one speaker asked, write of the past
in terms of a twentieth-century "frame of reference"? The
meeting decided that to do so was legitimate.

For myself, sitting watchfully in the audience between
two scholars, there was outrageousness in this discussion. It
was one of the games men play. Word games, very dangerous
to art and the artist. . . . Should historians look on the past
through the eye of the present, and was such a view legitimate?
*"In God's name, gentlemen, not only legitimate but inevitable!
What other view can there be?"* I got to my feet and said so
in as many words. The professors laughed, applauded good-
naturedly — and returned to their argument.

Afterward, they congratulated me on speaking my mind.
We like to be challenged, they said. Then why, I wondered
privately, had no one taken up the glove when I flung it?
"Mrs. Bowen's humanism." So the professors referred to me,
later that day, placing me neatly in a niche and thus disposing
of me and my subjective relativism. How obliging are these
words and terms, how useful to the logical mind! She is a
humanist, she is a relativist, she is a technocratic rationalist.
If I were not careful, I too would begin to talk this way.
Indeed, I caught myself at it that very evening, after the President of the Historical Association had delivered his address.
Leaving the hotel dining room with three professors I heard
my voice raised, with theirs, in praise, "Yes," I said. "Dr. R——
has a nice proportionate understanding of his function as a
teacher."

The professors nodded agreement, one of them even

repeated my words. "A nice proportionate . . ." Had I really said that? One more day at the convention and I would be referring to a good idea as a conceptual scheme, an outline of my current Adams chapter as a methodology, tomorrow's program as an agenda and the muse of history herself as a discipline. It was indeed anesthetic, this talk. At a morning assembly I had seen three professors sound asleep, one of them sitting in my row, another on the platform in plain sight of everybody. No one seemed to mind; falling asleep apparently was recognized procedure. My notes for that morning contained the words, scrawled large, addressed to heaven knows whom, "Sluggard on the left, awake!" And lower on the page, for my right-hand neighbor, "I don't want to seem pushy, but haven't we heard this speech before?"

Dr. Oliver Wendell Holmes, father of the Justice and himself a Harvard professor, once remarked that there was an insulating quality to the professor's chair which cut him off from the main currents. I challenged it; from my observation the professors were closer to life than most so-called practical men. Yet there was indeed a remoteness here, a quality almost of dream. On the mezzanine floor, among book exhibitions, a voice forever paged some lost character. "Mr. Bloomer," it called. "Mr. Bloomer, Mr. Bloomer."

Perhaps I only imagined the remoteness; somewhere within practical bounds no doubt there was a Mr. Bloomer, complete with head, hands and spectacles. Or do we always tend to call that remote which is not our own life, our point of view? Maybe I was a bit dazzled by academic verbiage, choked by it, like the man who had been to a feast of languages and stolen the scraps. The professors' concern was truth in history. Truth, they implied, is found through caution. *"Testing, testing!"* — through all their platform speeches the words seemed to sound like a refrain.

But there were other ways of coming at truth, I thought, and other ways of communicating it. Sir Francis Bacon wrote to King James I, one day, recommending with characteristic circumlocution a plan for controlling an approaching Parliament. "It may be it is an over-dilligence," Bacon said, "but still methinks there is a middle thing between art and chance: I think they call it prudence."

In post-Revolutionary days a portrait painter came to Philadelphia, a fugitive from France and the Terror. His name was Saint Memin and he drew America's great-grandfathers in pinkish crayon, always in profile. He did them with an instrument he called a "physionotrace," with which he measured nose, width of forehead, length of chin before he began to draw. I had found two portraits of John Adams by Saint Memin, one in a repair room of the Metropolitan Museum and one at a private house in New York's East Sixties. I had stared long at these pictures. Under a massive brow the eye was bold and prominent, cheeks heavy to coarseness; every feature suggested strength, stubbornness, intelligence. And the nose! It was powerful, prominent, worthy of the face; it was a beak. In other pictures I had seen this nose suggested. And I had studied, to be exact, some eighteen contemporary portraits of John Adams. From the Frick Art Reference Library on Fifth Avenue to the Antiquarian Society in Worcester, Massachusetts, I had combed the files for likenesses of what the catalogues called "Adams, J." And now at last I knew this nose was true, *echt,* authentic. Saint Memin had not guessed but measured it, inch for half-inch of living flesh. I had the portrait photographed; on the back I jotted down dates and appropriate details, adding with a flourish, "Never doubt that nose again!"

I thought of Saint Memin as I sat with the professors. They too did their work and wrote their books with the physionotrace, or something like it. Length and breadth, one could trust to the result; the back pages of their volumes included all proof and all citation. At a glance, these gentlemen knew if the facts in a history book were valid. They even knew when one should trust an encyclopedia. I had recently acquired the old *Appleton's,* in six heavy volumes, bound confidently in red. A most useful work, completed in 1894, which included sketches of John Adams's early colleagues, whom I had been able to find nowhere else — forgotten lawyers like Oxenbridge Thacher, Jeremiah Gridley, James Putnam of Danvers, Massachusetts. I mentioned it to one of the professors and he grinned. "Yes," he said. "I use *Appleton's* myself. But watch out for it. They paid their authors by space. Somebody who needed money wrote fortyseven sketches of men who never existed."

A wicked man, that encyclopedist, I thought, and thoroughly depraved. Yet the professors could do with a touch of his flair. Looking about me at the conference I saw no other person, male or female, of my ilk; I was the only non-academic except for one or two professional writers who came to make speeches and fled as soon as they were done. I knew why they had fled. For writers, this was insidious company. If a biographer stayed too long he could be paralyzed, unable to proceed. The words *presentation, communication* — I had not heard them mentioned. Which of these men would take a morning to find a right ending for his written sentence, or a week to discover the best way of presenting a scene — say, John Adams's defense of the British soldiers after the so-called Boston Massacre in 1770? (Should one open in court, with witnesses talking and give the incidents of that fateful evening through their depositions? Or should the chapter begin with the "massacre" itself, the February night, a young moon showing, men gathering on street corners, and the British guard crossing from the barracks to their sentry boxes on the square?) To write the story had taken me three months, and not a moment of the time spent on research; that had been done beforehand. Simply, I had tried the scene backwards and forwards, using the flashback, straight narrative, indirect conversation, direct quotes and every technique in the repertory until the scene merged — or so I hoped — with its rightful impact, the power, suggestion and color it deserved.

"Don't try to write for the general public," one professor cautioned from the platform. "If you do, you will fall on your faces. Write for your colleagues in the physics department." An honest man, and I honored him for it. But there were others not so candid, who intimated that style was a matter of tricks, to be acquired by anyone who chose to take time off from more important duties. . . . Tricks? — I thought, sitting there looking at my feet. Style is not tricks. Style is breath, *pneuma, spiritus* — the ancients had a word for it. If style is a trick then the transfusion of blood is a trick — a neat pouring of the life fluid from one container to another. Prayer too is a trick — a setting of the knees squarely on the floor, a bending of the head, a covering of the face so that water will not run from the eyes. . . .

Perhaps all this was no fit matter for argument. Like faith, perhaps these things required no more than acknowledgment, and the man who rejected them belonged merely in another camp. Maybe the historians should be divided into two groups, like English solicitors and barristers, one to collect and collate, and one to write the brief and present it in public. I had always admired Carl Becker, for many years professor of history at Cornell. His book, the *Declaration of Independence*, was my guide and inspiration; I knew bits of it by heart and liked to say them to myself. Here was a clean crisp style with energy to it, and a wonderful play of imagination upon the past. "As for you," Charles Beard had written to Becker, "I have heard on good authority that you are no *H*istorian; nothing but a *M*an of *L*etters. It makes me jealous."

I do not know how it might be managed, but I could wish the young scholar be given time to browse and roll in the best literature and language, before he feels the academic bridle. I have sometimes thought that a course in Jane Austen might help where a course in historiography only hinders. Walter Bagehot has remarked on the tremendous advantage held by the scholar who has had a sickly childhood, which forced him into "the habit of desultory reading." S. T. Coleridge felt, he said, a great superiority over those who had not read, "and fondly read," fairy tales in their childhood. He thought they wanted a sense which he possessed, a "perception or apperception of the universe."

Was that what I missed, in the professional historians, an apperception of the universe — no less? It is said that the best histories have been written by amateurs, persons outside the academic fold. Yet this is not all true by any means, and the writer who takes such an attitude is a fool. But I wondered, in this connection, that I had seen so few trade-book publishers, here at the December convention. If I were a publisher I would haunt such places, looking for books to publish and men to write them. There had been one conspicuous exception. Mr. Alfred Knopf was to be seen prowling the mezzanine, dark head bent, bold dark eyes gazing at the book exhibitions, at the carpet or perhaps at his own inward inscrutable thoughts. One day he ran into me, full tilt, asked what in God's name I was doing here and how I figured my place in this assemblage?

Well, I said, hadn't he noticed the professors talking about *disciplines?* There was the discipline called history, there were the social science disciplines, and economic odds and ends. And then there were those nameless subjects outside the academic garden, referred to vaguely as "other disciplines."

"I am other disciplines," I told Mr. Knopf. And so, for that matter, was he. There are ways to come at history, I thought, pursuing my way down the hotel corridor. Let us say the professors come at it from the northeast and I from the southwest. Either way will serve, provided the wind blows clean and the fog lifts.

Biographers do well, as I have said, to seek this company, though it can be dangerous; it can dislocate, interrupt, dam the flow and stop the story. To look at life and facts through the clear narrow lens of *academia* — it is another viewpoint altogether. What a man cannot name he cannot know: I have met the attitude not only in historians but outside the convention, in scientists, lawyers, judges on the bench. These are the confident men, the experts, the challengers, quoters of fact — impatient, quick and devastating. The writing of any long book is beset with obstacles, interruptions sought or unsought; the professional learns to surmount them. But there is a kind of interruption that is hard to describe — a breaking of the chain, an obliteration of the picture by a hand of doubt that sweeps purposefully across the writer's vision, a glancing blow that does not fell but temporarily blinds.

These effects can be achieved only by experts, persons whom the writer believes to be exceptionally knowledgeable. The adversary may be a brilliant intellectual or a mere stranger who steps into one's path. In the end the effect is good, provided the writer survives it. The act of confronting danger is exhilarating and makes for extraordinary effort: a man can jump a chasm if he is after tiger, or if a tiger is after him.

Among the species *academicus,* or expert, the most redoubtable and engaging specimen of my experience was Justice Frankfurter, literary executor of Justice Holmes and, as everyone knows, a professor of law at Harvard for twenty-five years before he went on the Supreme Court. If ever I met a challenger, it is that man. He was born to challenge, and in no ordinary way. I think the young lawyer fortunate on whom this shadow falls, provided he can survive eclipse. Frankfurter's questions cut down through easy thinking. I know, because I have felt the edge of that blade.

During the writing of *Yankee from Olympus,* I heard from Justice Frankfurter only at intervals. He had not wanted me to write the book and said so in no obscure terms; he had his own choice of biographer. I had known Justice Frankfurter, as it happens, since my youth; my sister and brother knew him. While I was writing, the messages he sent used to put me into a rapid boil. In the night I would wake and remember them; at times they brought me out of bed to walk the floor. He had heard, the Justice wrote under date of June, 1943, that I had been in Washington recently, in the Supreme Court building. Marshal Waggaman had told him I left some unsolved queries. "I'm answering for Mr. Waggaman. You both surprise and delight me — surprise me, that is, that you should not rely on your imagination for your facts but actually make efforts to attain accuracy. Are you ceasing to become an artist and becoming merely a thinker?"

It was wonderful and awful and I would not take diamonds for those letters and messages. They came seldom, but when they came they were noteworthy. "What are you going to do about the big cases — the *Lochner* case, the *Gitlow* case, *Rosika Schwimmer?* Without training in the law, surely you're not going to include the big cases? It makes my blood run cold." This was not written but spoken to me, face to face, at the outset of my work. And if the notion as expressed made the judicial blood run cold, it made mine run very hot indeed; the steam it generated was enough to drive me through the most difficult chapter in the book. If I had that biography to do again, I would not choose to do it without those notes and messages. Always they were to the point, they stung where I was tenderest. And what business has a writer, being tender? None at all. Tender toward his subject he should be, forever receptive, skinless indeed and open to every breath of suggestion that may come his way, but hard and resistant to the outside world.

Defiance! That was the key word. Thomas Carlyle had called upon it when he was writing his *French Revolution.* "The great difficulty is to keep oneself in the right balance, not despondent, not exasperated; defiant, free and clear." Justice Frankfurter's disapproval was heavy artillery. And there was no dodging it, one stood and took the blows. I would finish that book, I told myself, if it was my last action on earth.

I would get my facts correct and then write each episode, each legal case as I chose to write it. In the end I would submit my manuscript to whomever I wished, before publication, and withhold it from whom I wished. And if, in thirty-eight chapters as planned, I did not succeed in bringing to life that laurel-wreathed hero, O. W. Holmes, Jr., then I would try it in fifty chapters or in sixty.

I do not recall what I wrote back to Justice Frankfurter. I think it was polite and noncommittal and that the body of my rage went direct to the pages of my book, where it belonged, transmuted into something more serviceable. And was that the effect the Justice had planned? I thought about it, later. Twelve years after the book was published, Justice Frankfurter and I stood together on a public platform in Washington. We were there at his suggestion; he knew I was to lecture in the Theater of the Folger Library and greatly to my surprise had told the Director of the Library that he would like to introduce me. Much water had run under the bridge; my biography of John Adams had appeared, and of Sir Edward Coke. Yet I did not know if Justice Frankfurter had read them, or if he approved. I did not, in short, have a notion what was going to happen.

Justice Frankfurter got up, stood forward to the footlights and with immense vigor announced that I had written some eight books — he had sent to the Congressional Library for them and had read all but one. That one he still thought better not to read. He had done what he could to prevent my writing it. Mrs. Bowen, he said, would confirm this statement. The Justice turned, looked piercingly at me where I sat on the platform, grinned, and returned to the business at hand. There were people, he went on, who worked better under difficulty, and I was one of them. "I stand here," he told the audience, "I stand here to make public amends." He went on to use the word apology, but he need not have used it. What he said that night I shall always remember; it touched me closer than his strictures ever had. And after the battle, need the disputants prove the blows? A duel is a duel and keeps fighters on their toes, where fighters should be.

Professors, lawyers, judges — the experts have challenged me through many years, on many fronts. While I was writing John Adams's biography I was challenged, one evening, by a historian who said that my view of Adams was romantic altogether and he did not hold with it. George Washington only went into the army in 1754 to recover his lands along the upper Shenandoah Valley; didn't I know *that?* And the men who wrote our Constitution were merely trying to protect their property from the encroachment of the lower classes. He wasn't quoting Beard, the professor said; he didn't have to, the thing went further than Beard. He reminded me that John Adams himself liked to talk about "the poorer sort of men," or "the better sort," and that Adams was not referring to character but to economic status.

I could answer that professor today. I think I could have answered him then, but I was shy, not yet practiced in the arts of confrontation. I went home and wrote to Bernard De Voto in Cambridge, to tell him what had been said. I give his answer, entire:

"Sure you're romantic about American history. What your professor left out of account was the fact that it is the most romantic of all histories. It began in myth and has developed through three centuries of fairy stories. Whatever the time is in America it is always, at every moment, the mad and wayward hour when the prince is finding the little foot that alone fits into the slipper of glass. It is a little hard to know what romantic means to those who use the word umbrageously. But if the mad, impossible voyage of Columbus or Cartier or LaSalle or Coronado or John Ledyard is not romantic, if the stars did not dance in the sky when the Constitutional Convention met, if Atlantis has any landscape stranger or the other side of the moon any lights or colors or shapes more unearthly than the customary homespun of Lincoln and the morning coat of Jackson, well, I don't know what romance is. Ours is a story mad with the impossible, it is by chaos out of dream, it began as dream and it has continued as dream down to the last headline you read in a newspaper, and of our dreams there are two things above all others to be said, that only madmen could have dreamed them or would have dared to — and that we have shown a considerable faculty for making them come true. The simplest truth you can ever write about our history will be charged and surcharged with romanticism, and if you are afraid of the word you had better start practicing seriously on your fiddle."

7

John Adams's Bowl

The bowl sat on a pedestal in the middle of the auction gallery. There was no glass over it, no lock or key. Big and round and fragile and cobalt blue, with the shield on one side. "Diameter 14 inches," the catalogue said. "Script initial J [for Jefferson] surmounted by a helm, and having a banderole with motto *Rebellion to Tyrants is Obedience to God*. Lowestoft pitcher *en suite*. Both bowl and pitcher are understood in the family to have been given by Thomas Jefferson to President John Adams."

There was no need to consult the catalogue, I knew it by heart. Had I not studied it over and over while stretched on a bed of influenza? For ten days the catalogue had not left my side. Every object pictured, from the genealogy on page one to the Early Federal Mahogany Card-Table on page thirty-nine, was a matter of passionate interest. Two ladies, living in the environs of Boston and bearing names in which figured the words Adams and Quincy — these ladies were selling off, in one grand gesture, a big crowded roomful of furnishments that would cause watering in the mouth of every antiquarian, collector, and museum director from here to what John Adams would have called the Western Waters.

By day and by evening I had been pursuing Adams J. and Adams J. Q. with their relatives, connections and ramifications. For three years I had scarcely read a piece of print that was not concerned with the family; I had worked my way back through the Henrys and the Charles Francises until even their handwriting was familiar. Charles Francis's Civil War prose bade fair to blind me. John Adams had died on July Fourth, 1825 — the very jubilee, the fiftieth anniversary of Independence. Thomas Jefferson died on that same day. There was a glory in this double departure that needed no rhetoric. "The setting sun," wrote Charles Francis, "spread its rays over even the dispersing sky." Mr. Adams's last words, "so far as they could be gathered from his failing articulation, were these: 'Thomas Jefferson still survives.' "

Survives? John Adams never said survives. He said *lives,* he must have said it. He was dying. And besides, he was always a bluff talker. Not "refined" except, as he would have said, in morals. A blunt man, passionate, willful, vain. Honest to the farmer-Puritan marrow of his well-covered bones. And a patriot "as disinterested," Jefferson said, "as the being who made him."

The trouble was, I had been too much shut in libraries, this twelvemonth, let alone beds of influenza. Writing biography, like the practice of archeology, has its indoor and outdoor work cycles. I must go again to Braintree. I must see what was left of the Smith house in Weymouth over the hill, where Adams rode to court his Abigail. I must spend another week in Worcester, where John taught school. . . . I would begin now, next week, as soon as I was able, and visit every monument, every museum and gallery, every local historical society that possessed Adams relics, Adams prints, Adams furniture, Adams anything. I would get out my folder marked *Things to do* and start at the top of the list.

It was an exhilarating thought. I bought a stopover ticket for Boston, planning to see the Adams exhibition in New York on the way. Never mind the actual auction, all I needed was the catalogue and a few quiet hours before the bidding opened. In the train from Philadelphia I had studied the pictures anew so that when I should walk into the gallery I would not be a mere admirer among *objets d'art,* I would know and recognize and there would be stirrings within me. The photographs were clear, every bit as inviting as I had imagined. . . . Gilbert Stuart portraits, three of them. Josiah Quincy, whom I loved; the third Josiah, the one that was President of Harvard, "at half-length seated in an upholstered chair." Mrs. Josiah — how handsome they were and how elegant! No blinking the fact that the Adamses had come up in the world when John married Abigail Smith, with her Quincy connections. John Adams had not done it by design, he was too honest for that. Yet he was no man to ignore such matters; at the Continental Congress Adams had been embarrassed by the worldly manners of the Virginia delegates, nervous lest the New Englanders shame their constituents with their provincialisms.

In the train I had thought of these things. . . . "Paul Revere teapot and stand." In the catalogue the teapot was enchanting and grave with its fluted sides, its plain straight spout; it *looked* like John Adams. The Tutor Flynt cup. But they couldn't be selling the Tutor Flynt cup? There it was, photographed back and front. Obverse and Reverse, the catalogue said. "Domed cover with a series of stepped ring moldings and finished with a knopped urn finial."

My goodness, I thought, what fancy language. A knopped urn finial. Tutor Flynt surely never heard of one. "With the inscription *Donum Pupillorum Henrico Flynt, 1718.*" Tutor Flynt was uncle to Dorothy Q. Very odd and much beloved, he had taught at Harvard fifty years. Father Flynt, his students called him. I had turned the pages — miniatures, furniture, laces, autographs. And at the end, with a full-page picture all to itself, the Lowestoft bowl.

The sale was on the fifth floor, the elevator man said. For no reason at all I had got off at the fourth and was lost immediately in a forest of Chinese furniture, French furniture, Victorian furniture. Scroll and gilt and tasseled ornament, curly sentimental children looking out of thick gold frames. I found the staircase and went up, my damp shoes squeaking. In the whole huge building there seemed to be nobody but me. Maybe, I thought, because it was raining; maybe because it was Monday morning.

At the top of the stairs I turned right, where a long room opened into the hall. And there it was, not twenty paces ahead on its pedestal. Jefferson's bowl, big and round and cobalt blue, with the shield facing me. I walked slowly to it and stood looking down. At the bottom, in the center, was a little gilded spray, deliciously faded. Circling the top edge was a pattern. "Diaper pattern," the catalogue said, "in underglaze cobalted blue pendented with fleur de lis. White lemon-peel glaze. Between the exterior sprays are two shields with blue and gold star borders and script initial J surmounted by a helm, and having a banderole with motto . . ."

I bent down. There was the shield and there, sure enough, the brave initial J, delicately traced. *Rebellion to Tyrants is Obedience to God.*

The emotion that swept me was absurd. What right had I to feel this way? I was not an Adams, a Quincy. I was not even a Randolph from Virginia. An attendant strolled in, a cheerful young Negro in a green suit with brass buttons. "Can I help you?" he asked. "No, thanks," I said, and added idiotically, "Is this the Adams-Quincy room?"

It was a Thurber question, a Stephen Leacock question. (Sir, is this the bank?) All round was evidence as familiar to me that Monday morning as the evidence of my own country threshold.

The room was oblong, softly lighted through a glass ceiling. From the wall Josiah Quincy looked down, handsomer even than in the catalogue. Mrs. Quincy young, and Mrs. Quincy old and very distinguished in coat and lace mantilla. A dashing, dark-haired young man whose name I had forgotten, as one forgets the names of one's cousins a generation past, but whose faces remain familiar.

Beyond the bowl, in a lighted case, were laces, wide sugary flounces of Brussels and Milan. Against black velvet their fragile patterns stood out. A garden with paths leading to a dolphin fountain. Urns and baskets of flowers, traced with delicate precision. Near me, gravely alone in its glass case, stood the Paul Revere teapot, its curved black handle worn bare. Directly across the room was the Tutor Flynt cup and at my right a long case full of silver. Bowls and basting spoons, an egg warmer, a soup ladle with a deep scoop and long, light-colored wooden handle — indubitably the pleasantest thing in soup ladles I had ever seen. I looked it up. *Number 31.* "George I Silver Rattail Soup Ladle made by Chas. Jackson (?), London, 1724. Length 17½ inches. Fine plain oval scoop with pointed rattail molded upon the reverse, the tapering shank inset with a long pearwood baluster handle."

I wandered back to the Lowestoft bowl. It drew me, its magic was strong. *Rebellion to Tyrants* . . . Was this Jefferson's own motto? Had he borrowed it from Benjamin Franklin? Or did it perhaps have something to do with Charles I? When I got home I would look it up.

So Jefferson gave this bowl to John Adams. But *when* did he give it? The air was thick with questions, and where could I find reply? Not from young Negro boys in green suits nor from the auction woman at the telephone desk. Obviously, the bowl did not change hands early, when Adams and Jefferson were in France. It must have been after 1800, after Jefferson's second administration, after Mr. Madison's War — along in the 1820's, when the Chinese trade was flourishing, when the two old men had resumed correspondence, prodded by Dr. Rush to a friendship now historic.

Of course! Jefferson must have sent the bowl from Monticello as a pledge, a token. *"Mr. Jefferson and I have grown old and retired from public life. So we are upon our ancient terms of good-will. . . . He wished to be President of the United States and I stood in his way. . . . But if I should quarrel with him for that, I might quarrel with every man I have had anything to do with in life:*

> *'I love my friend as well as you,*
> *But why should he obstruct my view.'"*

So John Adams had explained it, an old, old man, to young Josiah Quincy, and so Quincy had reported it.

The bowl, then, must have made the long journey from Monticello to Quincy, Massachusetts, by stage and coasting sloop and wagon. Or had Jefferson simply sent it by his own private express, with a note scribbled hastily, no copy taken? A Negro servant, easy in the saddle, making the journey in summer, following the winding dusty roads northward to where marsh water showed below the blue hills of Quincy.

So I stood dreaming, while somewhere a clock struck the hour. It would soon be time for me to go. I turned slowly round. Would I remember this room? Falling in love does not insure remembering. The satinwood desk and table, the silver, the portraits — could I keep with me this spare shining beauty? Among it all, not a superfluous line. There was elegance here and honesty; a way of living, of valuing, thinking — disciplined, austere yet somehow crowned with grace. Remote from Louis XV downstairs, remote from Queen Victoria. And remote — how far away — from 57th Street in the rain, where I was going.

Extraordinary, that the philosophy of a century could speak so loudly in the tongues of things! 1718: Tutor Flynt's cup was sturdy and plain as befitted an era when plank floors, carpetless, were good enough for anybody. Three generations later, and the Paul Revere teapot is delicately fluted, delicately engraved. Time now for decoration laid on sparely, by a craftsman's hand still humble with the nearness of a Puritan God.

In the gallery, someone spoke and I jumped. Two women had appeared from nowhere; they were standing by the

Quincy portrait. One of them had a lorgnette in her hand; she leaned to the picture, peering. I had met these ladies or their counterparts on Beacon Street in earlier days. They were tall, dressed in tweeds; they wore low-heeled over-shoes and there was that about them which spelled Adams-Quincy.

My heart bounded in my chest. Here at last would be the answers to my questions. These pleasing, distinguished ladies would know all about such furnishments; they could tell me why American Hepplewhite was so much more agree-able than English Hepplewhite. I myself had decided it was because living was harder in Massachusetts than in England; the weather was colder, the fight to exist more grim, and grimness chops down ornament. Or had it to do with techniques, with words like *knopped urn final,* and *brides picotées?*

The two women were talking; I caught names familiar to the Adams-Quincy legend. Perhaps these ladies were cousin to the fortunate, the fabulous owners of this magic that sur-rounded me! The lady with the lorgnette was speaking; her final words emerged vigorous, clipped with the accents of Beacon Hill and in that quiet room startlingly decisive. ". . . so she gave the house to her sister to save taxes."

Texas, she pronounced it. To save Texas. But these two ladies knew everything! They might even be able to tell me the date when Jefferson gave the bowl to John Adams. The lady with the lorgnette had turned; she walked straight toward me. "Can you tell me," she asked, "where can I find a catalogue for the Adams-Quincy sale?"

Quinzy. *Quinzy.* I pronounced it that way too, but always with an effort, as when in Boston I had learned to say A*biel*

Holmes, to rhyme with "style." I smiled. "Catalogue?" I repeated. "You can have mine. I don't need it. I know these things by heart, how they look, that is. But I'm not from Boston, I'm from Philadelphia. I have some questions. Could you please tell me who was the last owner of the Tutor Flynt cup?"

The lady looked me over, unsmiling. Above me, that is. Not through me but above me at a point on the opposite wall. "Thank you," she said. "But I believe I see some catalogues at the desk, through that door." She was gone, and her companion with her.

I could have torn her tongue from her throat and made it into hash for witches. She had hurt my pride, but hurt pride was not what moved me. That woman had shut me out. Until this moment I had belonged, the room was mine and everything in it. By the grace of heaven, perhaps also by virtue of grubbing in libraries, long days of search, I, a stranger to the Parke-Bernet Galleries, had walked upstairs to this room and immediately I had been part of it.

In the next room the telephone rang at the desk. I turned again to the room, the cup, the teapot, the portraits and the bowl. It was as I had feared. They sat staring, cold, unfriendly. Tagged and numbered: 64, 65, 31. A sense of the past — is it then compounded wholly of illusion, so brittle, so easily broken and marred? Once I had been to Russia and brought illusion home with me. Searching for Justice Holmes I had fronted the denizens of Beacon Street and had not been routed. What business had a biographer, then, to be so vulnerable, so eternally thin-skinned where her subject was concerned — was I never to outgrow it?

There was no time to answer; thinking could come later.

Oh, might that woman burn in hell and all her children's children with her. Damn her eyes and teeth, her lights and liver!

She had come back, and brought the Negro boy with her. They stood by the Tutor Flynt cup; the boy unlocked the case and the woman took the cup in her hands. The motion brought me to my senses. But of course — this wasn't a museum, this was an auction gallery! We could touch these things, handle them; they were for sale. I turned and walked to the next room. The auction woman was telephoning, I leaned across the desk. *"Number 64,"* I said. "Could I have the sale estimate? Adams-Quincy heirlooms."

The girl nodded, thumbing expertly through a pile of papers, the receiver still quacking at her ear. *"Number 64 —* here it is," she said. "Lowestoft bowl. Fifteen hundred dollars. *Number 65,* pitcher to match. Seven hundred and fifty dollars."

"And *31,*" I added quickly. "A soup ladle. Could you please tell me . . . ?"

"Hundred and fifty dollars," the auction woman said.

I thanked her. There was a telephone booth in the hall, I couldn't get there fast enough. Eight blocks south was the office of my literary agent. I would call him and adjure him to come to this sale on Saturday and buy that ladle if he had to outbid the Metropolitan Museum and all the Adams-Quincy ladies in New England. My eye was filled with a picture of my agent — a New Hampshire man and good at trading — outbidding the two ladies. What if bidding for soup ladles was not the business of a literary agent? I dialed and waited. I felt wonderful.

"Hello, Harold!" I shouted. "I'm at an auction gallery. Listen, there's a soup ladle here. I want you to come up and bid on it, Saturday. Can you do that, will you be in town? It's Number 31. Have you got a pencil? A hundred and fifty dollars, asking price."

"Soup ladle?" my agent said. "*Soup* ladle! Where in God's name are you? I thought you were in Philadelphia. You didn't say a hundred and fifty dollars, did you? You can't afford a hundred and fifty dollars for a soup ladle."

But I was ready for that one. "A hundred and fifty dollars is nothing at all," I said loftily. "What I really *need* here is a bowl. A Lowestoft bowl that costs fifteen hundred dollars. And maybe a pitcher to go with it at seven hundred and fifty."

There was a pause. "I think I'd better come up there right away," Harold said. He sounded tired. "Where did you say you were? Now, don't move from that booth. Just sit quietly and don't —" his voice rose — "don't talk to anybody until I get there."

Talk to anybody! The trouble was, nobody would talk to *me*. "Oh, never mind," I said bitterly and with finality. "Never mind. Just forget the whole thing. I'm catching a train for Boston. Good-by."

I hung up and wandered down the hall. There were people coming and going now; the Adams-Quincy room buzzed with talk and movement. Those two men in overcoats were, plainly, commercial dealers. Their talk was swift and professional; they had jewelers' glasses with which they examined, not the portraits but the frames; they ran their fingers over the inlay on the satinwood desk, calling to each other across the room. They paid no slightest attention to anybody. I stood a moment in the doorway, my heavy coat trailing from one shoulder.

The auction woman came from her desk, walking swiftly, purposefully to the bowl. She had someone in tow, a woman in a beret, with a notebook and pencil in her hand. The woman with the notebook said loudly, "There is a crack in this bowl."

The auction woman shook her head. "Those are age cracks."

"No," the other said. "No! This long crack. It goes all the way across, don't you see? The bowl has been broken and mended. Mended all the way through."

By now I was standing with them. The auction woman reached out and flipped the bowl with thumb and forefinger. And the bowl sang, sent out a clear, calm protest that died briefly on the air.

"That crack," I asked. "Will that crack bring down the price?"

The auction woman shook her head. "Wouldn't think so. Historic piece. Belonged to Thomas Jefferson." She flipped it again. "Hear that?" she said. "Wonderfully clear, isn't it?"

She stooped, peering. "Rebellion to tyrants . . ." she read slowly, spelling it out, *"Rebellion to Tyrants is Obedience to God.* . . . No, that crack won't bring down the value."

The two women walked away. It was time for me to go, too, but I could not go. There was a chair outside the door in the hallway, in full sight of the room. With my coat and umbrella and handbag in a bunch on my lap, I sat down. People strolled by; the elevator door clanged. The two dealers moved past me, their hats on their heads, the jewelers' glasses hidden away. At the stairway they stopped. "Bidding's going to be brisk Saturday," one of them said. "The portraits will be slow but there's already been two bids on that Lowestoft bowl. Number 65 goes with it, the pitcher. Personally I think they've estimated too low on the pitcher. It'll bring twelve hundred if it brings a cent."

Beyond, down a brief flight of stairs, I could see the auction room with the stage and rows of chairs, waiting for Saturday. What, I wondered wearily, was this about possession? It had never troubled me before. Two hours in the place and I had persuaded myself that I owned the bowl, the pitcher, the soup ladle, Josiah Quincy and his lady, the Paul Revere teapot, the lace flounces with the urns and the fountain.

Why was I so greedy? I had never owned a piece of old Lowestoft in my life. I had never, in fact, especially wanted to own one. Nor had I collected anything, either Hepplewhite or Sheraton; in our house we sat on the chairs that had belonged to Aunt Eliza or we went out and bought something comfortable. There was no use in taking too high a tone; after all, I had never owned the Winged Victory, or "Venus Rising from the Sea." Beauty, says the philosopher, is in the eye of the beholder. Was it not, then, as splendid merely to walk through this gallery or that museum — to look upon beauty and pass on, unpossessing?

No! It was not as splendid. The bowl — that was Jefferson's bowl. John Adams's bowl. If I had it I could look at it every day. I would put it in the center of my small dark dining-room table, and each time I passed through the room I could look down into it and see the faded gilt branch in the middle. I would stoop, and under the shield

I could read the motto. Passing, I could put out my hand and touch it.

Sitting in the bleak hallway I argued thus with myself, while downstairs, lights went on in the auction room. Odd, that I had walked by this morning without seeing that theater; the door on the landing must have been closed. Or was it my mind that had been closed, refusing to realize this was a sale? Not a poem or a temple but a sale. These things were here to be dispersed. Somebody needed money and would sell; somebody had money and would buy. And who was I to make an angry moral issue of it?

I had walked into the Adams-Quincy room this morning cautiously, getting off the elevator at the floor below on purpose — I knew it now — so that I could come at these things slowly, find them myself by virtue of recognition, not be led by a crowd. I had hoped merely to recognize a portrait, a bowl, a cup. And I had walked wide-eyed into — what? An illusion, a dream more real than reality. Over that threshold I had stepped into another place, another century — the very place and time I had been seeking on the dry shelves of libraries.

Immediately, the room had been mine, with no need to touch or buy. But of course! I saw it now. Does one buy a friend, a daughter? And by that same token, does one lose a friend at the first threat, the first hobgoblin with frosty Boston manners? What I needed this morning was not an agent to bid on bowls but a philosopher to teach me reason. *Possession!* It was a difficult concept, not to be defined single-handed; it raised questions not to be answered by the likes of me. But all the same, if beauty was in the eye of the beholder, might not possession be there also?

I pulled my coat and handbag up on my lap and leaned forward, looking straight into the Adams-Quincy room. At this lunch hour it was empty save for the two young Negroes in their green suits with brass buttons, smart yellow stripes down their trouser legs. How well they suited the room; they looked just right, standing there. In knee breeches and white stockings they would look even righter. How quiet it all seemed and how beautiful. It was good to sit here alone, with the people gone. What was it John Adams used to write in his diary, back in the 1760's before the fighting began, when Britain and America were, as he said, staring at each other? "I will stand collected within myself and think upon what I read and what I see."

I got up, put my things carefully on the chair and made ready to go. Better not miss that train to Boston. At the elevator I rang the bell. "Got off at the wrong floor, didn't you?" the elevator man said. I told him yes, but I had found my way all right.

8
Biographer's Holiday

The end of his book comes unexpectedly upon an author. And this is odd, considering that for months, perhaps years, he has been anticipating the moment with almost pathological anxiety. He has been sure that he would die before his work was done, and being in palpably good health throughout, he has not liked to confess this anxiety. The feeling, however, is common to artists; psychologists I believe have a name for it. With Peter Tchaikovsky it took the form of being certain, before conducting a concert of his own music, that his head would fall off during performance — an awkward situation because conducting requires two hands, with none to spare for holding down the head.

There is an element of usefulness in this despair; it has a driving force. "I have no hope of my book, except for being done with it." So Carlyle, in the midst of writing his *French Revolution* — "that smoke and flame conflagration." With a long book, a history or biography, the anxiety is exacerbated.

"Matter multiplieth toward the conclusion," said old Thomas Fuller, apologizing for delay in completing the last of three volumes. Yet somehow the day arrives. Somehow, here it is, a sleeting Tuesday at twelve noon and one's book is done, over with, finished and in the mail, addressed to the publisher. In one's study the big desk is bare and the bookshelves above the desk; volumes from public libraries have been returned.

This freedom, this space and celestial roominess is not quite believable; there is a sensation of extraordinary well-being, as in convalescence or escape after dangerous accident. What is to be done with all this time, this delicious sudden gift of hours? Winter and summer, seven days a week, one had wakened to a self-imposed discipline as strict, hour for hour, as a nun's. Clocked and rigid, one had lived and moved in an alien time, a place and century not one's own. After five years of work on *John Adams and the American Revolution,* for me the sensation was particularly strong. By the time 1950 came around, the daily journey backward in centuries had become habitual, I could not do without it. I busied myself in looking through my notes, I agitated myself over fancied omissions and commissions. Much good material had been abandoned for lack of space. The writing of a long biography invariably means a series of eliminations, agonizing to the author, including plans for special research as time grows shorter.

Beyond Philadelphia, most of my reading for Adams had been done, quite naturally, in Boston and Cambridge. But I had been greatly tempted to further journeys — to the Clements Library at Ann Arbor, Michigan; the Newberry in Chicago, the John Carter Brown Library at Providence, Rhode Island. Not only did these famous repositories contain material pertinent to the eighteenth century, but they harbored librarians of talent and parts, known to scholars everywhere. I had wanted to meet these men and talk with them. They would know the names, people, places with whom and with which I had become familiar. They would respond to news about these men and women, long dead, who had been my intimate companions every day, yet whom I could never discuss, upon emerging from work, because nobody near me had shared the journey backwards in time. Twice, during the writing of my book, I had sent letters to Randolph Adams at Ann Arbor, asking if I might come and see him. After all, it had been his little treatise, *Political Ideas of the American Revolution,* that first interested me seriously in John Adams. Randolph had replied warmly to my letters, but I had given up Ann Arbor because the last months of my contract were expiring, the material already threatened to overwhelm by its bulk and I could not expose myself to more.

It came over me, suddenly, that I could now go anywhere I chose. My completed manuscript was in the publishing house at Boston. The Book of the Month judges, I was told, planned to read it in typescript, not wait for galleys. This meant weeks or perhaps months of delay, when I should be neither in my book nor wholly out of it. Impossible to begin a new project or even to think of one; the notion was abhorrent, next thing to a betrayal. On the telephone I complained bitterly to my publisher. Did he appreciate the discomforts of the no man's land to which I was condemned? How long must a person endure this half-and-half existence?

"Why don't you go away somewhere?" my publisher suggested. "Take a little trip. Fly off and see those libraries you are always talking about."

There was no question of flying. All booklovers, I think, like to ride on trains; the situation is at once soothing and conducive to reading. A seat by the window, a volume on one's knee and, as eyes tire, the country rushing by, strange scenes toward which one has no responsibility, a far horizon one has not seen before. A friend had given me a black linen bookstrap, hairy enough to cling to slippery covers, equipped with a self-fastening buckle and a loop to go over the shoulder. Into it I tied four hard-cover books, two from a nearby college library and two that I owned. The corners of my suitcase neatly held four paperbacks. "A busman's holiday," my husband said, observing these preparations. "I thought you were finished with John Adams and the eighteenth century."

"I want to talk about John Adams," I told him. "I want somebody to talk to *me*."

I felt blithe, full of high expectancy. Merely because one no longer needed historical material was no reason for not going out and enjoying the sight of it. Now at last, I could read without a pencil in my hand. I could range the library shelves, take down old books and page them through without so much as a glance at the index under *A, for Adams*. The Clements Library had a number of soldiers' letters, written in Nova Scotia during the siege of 1745 against the French; I had seen them in the catalogue. John Adams was ten when Massachusetts men sailed north to train their guns against that famous fortress. I must see these letters, among other things, though I knew my book had no space to hold them.

I wrote ahead to Randolph Adams in Ann Arbor and to Dr. Lawrence Wroth at the Brown Library and launched myself first toward Providence, Rhode Island. According to its Directors' Reports, the John Carter Brown Library specialized in "Americana to 1801." What, for me, could be more pertinent? I had much enjoyed Dr. Wroth's little volume, *An American Bookshelf, 1755*. Here was a scholar's treatise that flowed like a song. And what an excellent notion, for the author to pretend he was a reader in the year 1755, then choose books from the shelf, and discuss them! Somewhere I had seen a list of Dr. Wroth's publications: titles ranging from "The Indian Treaty in Literature" to "The Chief End of Book Madness" and "Mystical Reflections on the Ampersand." From these I had formed a picture of Lawrence Wroth. He was going to be tall, lean, blue-eyed, with beautiful remote eighteenth-century manners, a courtly bow as I entered his office.

I went up nine gray stone steps to the Library, crossed a room lined with handsome, leather-bound volumes and was introduced to a man of medium height, broad-shouldered, compact, with large dark eyes behind steel-rimmed spectacles. His smile was brief though kind, his air vague as he welcomed me and asked what I had come especially to see? Actually, it was the first time I had entered a research library without a plan, a definite and rather intense bibliographical aim. So I told Dr. Wroth I had come to see *him,* which was true, and that I was interested in anything he cared to show me.

"Indian treaties?" Dr. Wroth asked, at once.

Indian treaties were about the last thing I had been thinking of. I had never seen an Indian treaty, I had no desire to see more than one. Dr. Wroth, it soon became clear, was working on these at the moment. Before I knew it, I was sitting alone at a long table in the empty reading room, perusing Indian treaties. Dr. Wroth had vanished into cellar or attic, some guarded quiet place of his own. He would be back at one, he had said, to take me to lunch.

For an hour, I sat and looked at Indian treaties. . . .

"We will brighten the Chain, and strengthen the Union between us; so that we shall never be divided, but remain Friends and Brethren as long as the Sun gives light; in confirmation whereof, we give you this Belt of Wampum.

"Which was received with the Yo-hah."

The what? I asked myself. Ah, here it was, in a footnote: "The Yo-hah denotes Approbation, being a loud Shout or Cry, consisting of a few Notes pronounced by all the Indians in a very musical Manner, in the Nature of our Huzza's."

I tried it, softly, first in major and then in minor. Yo-o-Hah! What a pity not to know the tune! So Indians really did talk like Hiawatha. No wonder Dr. Wroth had wanted to see these documents in print, properly annotated. Yet for my part I have never liked to think about American Indians. I am not proud of the way we have behaved toward them and I would rather read about something else. John Adams, as I recall, did not like to think about Indians either; he once refused to work on an Indian Commission. I should have known better than to come here without queries and a plan. Librarians who are writing books on Indian treaties cannot be bothered with ladies who enter their door in mid-morning, aimless and enthusiastic. A librarian is not, after all, a museum man. And even if he were, he could not attend to every undirected curiosity that came up the steps and through the hallway.

Within reach on the table was a samll volume entitled *The John Carter Brown Library*. It proved to be a centennial speech that Dr. Wroth had made, some years before. I read it from cover to cover; I did not know a centennial speech on anything, let alone libraries, could have such charm. There was a young man in the speech named Henry Stevens, who in mid-nineteenth century had begun to help Mr. Brown to collect his books and who styled himself "Henry Stevens of Vermont." This Henry Stevens of Vermont, with whom I fell in love at first mention, went to England to buy books, then became a book trader and settled down in London. Not to be outdone by the gentry, he commenced adding capital letters after his name, "Henry Stevens, G.M.B., B.B.A.C." *Green Mountain Boy,* the letters signified; and, in memory of an incident from which he carried scars, *"Black Balled Athenaeum Club."*

The book carried me forward a good half hour. Then I got up and walked around the room, examining the shelves. Settling on Ralegh's *Discovery of Guiana,* I marked the space where it belonged, carried it to my seat and read until five minutes of one, when I returned the volume to its niche.

I cannot remember, from a distance of years, how it was at lunch, what we ate or talked about. I recall only that it was agreeable, I was glad that I had come. But I knew also that when Dr. Randolph Adams, at the Clements Library in Michigan, should inquire, next Tuesday, why I was there and what I wanted to see, I would be prepared. In my hand would be a list of titles; I would dream up something esoteric and difficult, to challenge his skill as librarian. *"Mrs. Bowen, what, especially, do you wish to see?"*

Whatever my answer, it would preclude Indian treaties.

At the door of their house in Ann Arbor, Dr. and Mrs. Adams met me, both talking at once. . . . What was my biography of John Adams to be called, had I a good title? And was it true that I had written it because of Randolph's little book, *Political Ideas of the American Revolution?*

It was indeed true, I replied. That superb brief treatise had sparked me off — a beautifully imaginative scholar's essay that said things never before hinted at, descriptive of John Adams's genius, his prophetic view.

Randolph Adams laughed, peering at me, where we stood in the hallway. He carried his head thrust a little forward, and though I believe he had been very ill, he gave an impression of eagerness, all his movements were quick. "Let's be done with formality," he said, "and call each other *Randolph."* There was no egotism to the way he said it. Plainly, the name could cover two people, and this generous vitality encompass a half dozen such as I. Where was my suitcase, he asked. At the hotel? Nonsense! Plenty of room right here in the house, if I didn't mind sleeping among a boy's books. Their two sons were grown up, away earning their livings. But Tom had kept his boyhood books. . . . Two days and nights, was that all the longer I planned to stay? How could anybody expect to see the Clements Library in two days and nights? It was *lèse-majesté, lèse-bibliothèque.*

I never had a better time or felt more at home. Every room in the Adams house was crammed with books. I had not been there twenty minutes before Randolph had untied my bookstrap, read the titles aloud, commented on their contents and inquired if this was all I had brought along to read? In another twenty minutes we were on our way to the Library. Accustomed, for years, to the genial shabbiness of historical societies and college reference libraries, I asked

Randolph if I was going to be awestruck by this place? It was, I had been told, a very palace of books. A shrine.

"*We* never go *in* the front door," Randolph replied. I wondered, was this an answer to my question? Back doors are traditionally modest. We went in and up the stairs, turned right and entered a room ninety feet long at the least, book-lined, with oak-paneled walls and a painted ceiling — the most luxurious library room I had ever seen. I followed Randolph through the building. The floors were of waxed hardwood, carpeted deep, my steps made no sound. We turned into still another handsome room, of medium size, with tall windows, carved paneling, a big table in the center, a solemn portrait of a gentleman in flashing collar and neat, discreet cravat. "The Treasure Room," Randolph said. He motioned toward the wall. "Founder and Donor. We'll see the books in a minute. The Board meets here. Why don't you say something?"

I had stopped short and was gazing at a portrait over the door. "Isn't that Tom Paine?" I asked. "What is he doing here," I made a gesture, "among all this?"

Randolph glanced up. "Salutary influence, having Tom preside," he said briefly. "Hung the picture myself. The rebellious corset maker. Trouble is, the Trustees don't recognize who he is."

Randolph took me into his office and sent for maps. Any biographer is perforce interested in maps; in my study I had not yet taken down the wall maps of Massachusetts, of Lexington, Concord, Boston, Braintree, Philadelphia. Some had been modern, some facsimiles of old ones. Now, spread on the desk or rolled out on the floor I saw original eighteenth-century maps and drawings from the famous Henry Clinton Collection, used by the British general in his American campaign. If a book in the original edition is evocative, how much more so a map, drawn on the spot in red ink and black, the streets with their old names and uncertain spelling. ... *"A New Plan of ye Great Town of Boston in America with Many Additionale Buildings, & new Streets, to the year 1769."*

Now, why had I not come sooner to this place, why hadn't I spent a year at the Clements, while I was writing about John Adams? I put the question to Randolph. "You would never have got done, that's why," he said, sensibly. "Wasn't it your hero, Holmes, who told his secretary, 'There comes a time, young feller, when a book has to be *finished*'?"

We put away the maps and returned to the Treasure Room, next door. The luxury of the building no longer drew my attention, the splendor of the books eclipsed it. We saw Hakluyt's *Voyages, Purchas his Pilgrimes,* De Bry's *Historia Americae.* Tall folios, bound in vellum, rich brown leather or scarlet morocco, gold-tooled. As Randolph talked, I sat and turned the pages on my lap. De Bry fell open to the picture of an Indian maiden, standing by a fire and gnawing happily at the shoulderbone of an erstwhile Spanish explorer, whose other limbs were dispersed gorily on the ground. "The book always comes open there," Randolph said. I saw the Columbus letter of 1493, printed in Latin. I saw Hariot's *Virginia,* Cabeza de Vaca's narrative, and the wonderful adventures of the incredible John Smith. . . .

Explorers, traders, missionaries, conquistadores. Before John Adams could clear his stony fields in Braintree, Massachusetts, these men had perforce to make their perilous journeys. Jesuit fathers in dugout canoes, pushing their paddles against wild water for the glory of God, in territory magnificent and unknown . . . *Terra incognita!* The words caught at my breath. Old Presbyterian that I am, I had the instinct to cross myself and say a Latin prayer.

Instead, I took out a handkerchief and blew my nose. Randolph leaned down to look at me. "Well!" he said. He sounded gratified. "Let's say the emotion does you credit."

In plain fact, this was not the first time I had seen a De Bry or even a Columbus letter. But I had never seen them with such a custodian at my elbow, talking, as the phrase goes, like an angel. Randolph Adams died a few years after my visit; that is, he left this earth. Does he stand now before some celestial bookcase, expounding to the winged and listening hierarchies the difference between a scholar and "a *mere* scholar"? If, among the seraphim, there is one who can out-talk him, I could lose a considerable bet with the seraphic head librarian.

I cannot recall, today, exactly how long I remained at Ann Arbor and the Clements Library. On the third or fourth morning, Randolph led me in the front way, past the yew trees, up the wide steps and through white columns. Near the door was a carved inscription. I read it aloud:

> *In darkness dwells a people*
> *That knows its annals not.*

A trifle bumpy as poetry, I thought; the accent a little comic on the word *not*. But true none the less, and descriptive of a situation that Randolph Adams and I were endeavoring, in our several ways, to improve. How fortunate for me, that Randolph was interested in John Adams and had written a book about him! My needs were fulfilled, here in this place; Randolph Adams talked about the eighteenth century as if he had been there yesterday and were going back tomorrow. No need to think up esoteric questions; Randolph was the one who questioned *me,* leading on from topic to topic and from year to year in history. He had even reached the present and asked about the progress of my book through the publishing house, what stage it was in at the moment, and why not remain here at the Library until I had news of the Book Club's acceptance or rejection? The publishers might then decide that I could make the book longer, include some of the material that I had sacrificed for lack of room. . . .

That same afternoon, I found myself sitting alone on the top floor of the Library in the manuscript division, reading soldiers' letters, written from Nova Scotia during the siege of 1745 against the French. Scrawled on soft, folded paper, spelled any which way, the patient, homesick words transported me to that bleak time and shore, cold, monotonous and lamentably remote from the towns and hamlets of Massachusetts. In spite of Randolph's suggestion, I knew that my Adams biography was already too long, the excerpts could not be used. Yet I did not want to lose them, somehow, and I began copying lines into my notebook: "Governor Sherley and Admiral Woran has declared we must Stay whilst the [British] troops arive so that we shall not Com hom this winter. P S we are all liveing and in pretty good helth Sir i ask your Good prairs. . . ." And from the Commander, Colonel Vaughan, "I have lived here in Great Bitternesse of

Mind and chearfully Done my Duty, at Ye same Time despised yt."

The manuscript division of the Clements Library includes
two rooms, light, bright, equipped with writing tables and a
telephone, and connected by an open archway. It was perfectly
still, up there, the floor entirely vacant. I had been reading
all day, my eyelids felt sandy. I finished with the letters and
began to think about the title to my Adams book. There had
been title trouble ever since I mailed the manuscript to Boston.
My three former biographies had sported fancy names — what
the book trade refers to as "selling titles." *Beloved Friend,
Free Artist, Yankee from Olympus.* None of these gave the
reader so much as a hint of the subject matter, a deception
which at the time had seemed to me indecent, a trick played
on the book buyer. I much preferred a plain, factual title;
say, *John Adams and the American Revolution.* This I had
suggested to my publishers, but they turned it down. No one,
they said, would buy a book with such a title; it was dry,
heavy, positively reader-repellent. I would have to find something better. "Something alliterative, snappy, eye-catching."

Thus spurred, I had taken up the Bible and read through
Proverbs and Ecclesiastes, hitherto fertile sources of book
titles, but this time barren. Bartlett's *Familiar Quotations* and
Justice Holmes's *Collected Speeches* had yielded a small harvest. In the end I must have submitted a dozen titles, and
something wrong with all of them. They had been used, or
they were five words instead of four or four instead of three.
Finally, I came up with *John Yankee,* from a letter John
Adams had written in 1778 to a friend in Massachusetts. He
said he used to call himself, with pride, John Bull. "But now
I am John Yankee." I did not like the title overmuch; it

seemed silly to publish two books with the word *Yankee* on the cover. But my publisher said it was perfect. We argued, settling finally on *John Yankee,* but with my original title printed directly underneath: *John Adams and the American Revolution.*

Now, months later, sitting on the top floor of the Clements Library, I thought of all this. *John Yankee,* indeed! It still made me uncomfortable. I saw myself starting a series, like the Rover Boys: *Yankee from Olympus . . . John Yankee . . . Yankees and Giants . . . Yanks and Pranks. . . .* I had told the librarians at the Clements about it; they showed gratifying interest and sympathy. Why was I so timid, Randolph had demanded. Why didn't I stand out for the title I wanted, was I going to let myself be dictated to? Publishers existed for the writer's convenience, not the other way around.

I wondered, now, about the time of day; my watch seemed to have stopped. It must be four o'clock at least. Tea time. Surely, somebody would come to the third floor and rescue me? I got up, found a wall clock. Five minutes to three.

For readers in libraries, perhaps for the world at large, this is the day's low point. Who was it said, "In hell it will always be three in the afternoon"? At three in the afternoon it requires a hero to sit and read manuscript. True, I had done it often, but only with a book in process, driven by a book, haunted by a book to the point where there are no heroics but only the urgent race before necessity.

In the next room, through the archway, a telephone rang, and rang again. Answering it was not my business and I knew it. Yet I rose and from sheer idleness hurried through the arch and picked up the receiver. "Boston, Massachusetts,

calling," the operator said. "For Mrs. Bowen." She pronounced it to rhyme with Cow.

It was my publisher. The Book of the Month, he said
jubilantly, had taken my biography for July publication. Eight
months off. "But they've changed the title," he added. "They
don't like *John Yankee*."

"They don't?" I said. I inquired if this meant I had to
start all over again with Ecclesiastes and Bartlett. My publisher
said no, the Book Club had a title. There was a slight but
perceptible change in his voice as he said it. I asked him,
what title?

"They're going to call it *John Adams and the American
Revolution*," he said.

"Yo-hah!" I said.

I hung up and ran downstairs, then through the long
hall as fast as I could go to the Librarian's Office, burst in
without knocking and told my news. Randolph jumped up
from behind the desk, seized my hands and held me at arm's
length, laughing with pleasure. The cataloguers next door,
hearing the commotion, hurried in. From here on my memory
is hazy. But in my mind there persists a picture — is it dream
or reality? — of Randolph waltzing me solemnly round the
office, still at arm's length, while the cataloguers beat time
and whistled.

9
Salute to Librarians

The pleasing condition known as true love is seldom attained without difficulty. Nowadays, I can declare with truth that I am in love with librarians — engaged in a perpetual, delightful affair of the heart with all public custodians of books.

But in my early twenties, struggling in library basements with bound volumes of newspapers or shuffling through a jungle of card catalogues, I was convinced that librarians existed solely to keep people from reading books. It is natural for young readers to experience shyness in big city or university libraries; the presence of so many books is at the same time exciting and intimidating. The young scholar longs for introduction, a knowledgeable hand to reach, point, act as intermediary between himself and all those riches.

In early days, I tried not to give librarians any trouble, which was where I made my primary mistake. Librarians like to be given trouble; they exist for it, they are geared to it. For the location of a mislaid volume, an uncatalogued item, your

good librarian has a ferret's nose. Give her a scent and she
jumps the leash, her eye bright with battle. But I did not
know this. All unaware I used to make my way to those
block-long municipal buildings, hope in my heart and in my
hand a list of ten or fifteen books. Not books to read in the
library but to take home, where I could copy at length, with
time to think about what I was copying. I did not telephone
beforehand and ask to have my books ready at the desk. I took
my list and looked up the proper numbers in the card catalogue, rechecked each one and carried the cards to the desk.
The young woman would glance at the cards and then she
would say, "Only two books at a time can be taken from the
circulation department, miss." Black hatred would then well
up in a heart that had been ready to love.

"Shut not your doors to me proud libraries." Walt Whit-
man had said it and the words gave comfort, letting me know
the great had their troubles, too, in libraries. But I was puz-
zled. Why should there be a conspiracy to keep anyone away
from books? The fault must lie in myself, perhaps in my lack
of systematized training in research. This was long before I
had met the professors or attended a conference of historians; there was still fixed in my mind the pleasing illusion
that the possessor of a Ph.D. in history has before him a blazed
trail, a path straight to the heart of his subject.

While I was working on the life of Tchaikovsky, in 1938,
a British musicologist happened to be a guest in my brother's
house. I admired Professor Dent's books about musicians; I
was sure that so famous a scholar could tell me how to proceed and that his experience would provide a magic formula
for libraries, an open sesame to those tall imperious doors.
I asked Mr. Dent point-blank how he went about his research.

(I was too inexperienced to know this is not a question one asks of scholars.) "Do you use five-by-eight cards?" I said. "How do you start, for instance?"

Mr. Dent smiled. "How do *you* start?" he asked. "How do you do your research?"

"Me?" I said. "Oh, I just plunge around in libraries."

Twenty-three years and five books later, I know that Mr. Dent answered me in the only way he could. On that tortuous long journey there is indeed no sure trail, no short-cut. I went ahead, plunging and bucking my way through libraries or slinking defeated from some municipal encounter. I do not know how it is with other students of history. But looking back, it seems my every forward movement derived not from success but failure, from some humiliation suffered, inducing anger, the stubborn resolve to find what I knew was on the shelves and use it in my own way for better or for worse.

One day in the New York Public Library, I received a crushing rebuff. That the incident was due to my own ineptitude made it, as usual, no easier to bear. I had walked into the Slavonic Division and told the learned curator that I was writing a life of Tchaikovsky. Might I look around, not at the cards but at the shelved books, the titles? "You speak Russian, of course?" the curator asked, with a fine roll of the R. His question took me by surprise. Actually, I knew enough to read titles and find my way about. But I gave a cautious negative. No, I didn't speak the language.

The curator shrugged. "No Russian?" he said. "Then of what use to come to this room? What use to write a life of Peter Ilich Tchaikovsky?"

I turned tail and fled, too flustered to stop and explain that I had a Russian collaborator, and that we both knew quite well what we were doing. At the Pennsylvania Station I boarded the train for home. By the time we reached Princeton Junction I had recovered. People, I thought, should be thrusting books at me, not snatching them away! Moreover, it was high time I did something to resolve this feud between me and the charge-out ladies and gentlemen behind the desks. The train pulled into North Philadelphia, and it came to me with a redeeming flash that what I needed to study was not books, systems, "disciplines," but *librarians*.

I bought a large notebook, something I am apt to do in moments of stress. Perhaps every student does it; a clean, untouched notebook invites the bravest plans. On the outside of this one I wrote "Librarians and Libraries," and then I began making lists of the librarians I had encountered. After each name I wrote a brief and useful characterization. The lists were continued for years, they were made in all seriousness, meant only for business, and they far overflowed that first notebook. I have them today and reproduce some samples, unchanged except for the exclusion of one proper name:

Library of Congress. Mr. Shaw — Mr. Cole. Can find anything. God's sakes don't forget your library number.
Harvard Archives. Mr. Lovett, wears glasses. Bright. Mr. Elkins, seventh floor, Widener. Head Man. Cannot understand what I am trying to do, but helpful. Said, "You don't want *printed* material, do you?" No use telling him why I want it. Just give him the numbers.
Widener Library downstairs. Mr. X . . . Old curmudgeon.

Hates women. Keep away from him. Find out name the little short one, desk, head of stairs. Sweet.

Massachusetts Historical Society. Mrs. Hitchcock, the nice one who knows Mr. Henry Adams. When he comes in the basement she will notify me upstairs. Says better not let him catch me downstairs near the Adams Papers. Says he takes off his hearing aid to make it harder. Says don't be put down by this. Says just yell.

This last was written in the late 1940's, before the Adams Papers, a superb repository of historical material, were thrown open to scholars. Mr. Henry Adams was custodian of the Papers, and only an occasional favored student was permitted a glimpse inside the room. Mr. Barnes's famous arcanum of paintings, near Philadelphia, was never more difficult to penetrate; I was forewarned to failure. Already there had been correspondence by mail and by messenger. At Mr. Adams's instance I had reduced my requests to specific queries. There were eight of these, carefully worded and typed; I had delivered them to Mr. Adams's office on State Street. What I wanted from the Adams Papers was modest enough; it had to do with John Adams at college, between 1751 and 1755. Adams's *Autobiography* had been printed nearly a century ago in what its editor called "fragments," opening with the year 1775; the Massachusetts Historical Society had printed a brief and still earlier "fragment" in which John Adams told of taking his entrance examinations for Harvard. It seemed to me there must be more, somewhere. Adams was deeply interested in education. Surely he would mention his teachers, his tutors? I counted on one more meeting with the curator of the Papers, here in the Historical Society. A last chance and I knew it.

I had been at work in the library for perhaps a week, when one morning Mrs. Hitchcock sent word that Mr. Henry Adams had entered the building and was on his way up in the elevator. The second floor of the Massachusetts Historical Society is a succession of handsome, open rooms that echo, with lofty doorways and marble floors. I stood perhaps ten steps from the elevator. Mr. Adams got out, took a startled look at me and snatched a hearing button from each ear. My instinct was for retreat but I advanced, and there in the open room gave tongue for a full half-hour. Mr. Adams had my list; I had a carbon. We stood and I shouted. Finally Mr. Adams seized me by the elbow. "Mrs. Bowen," he said, "I don't want to block your work. I don't want to be the cause of destroying your chapters, as you say I will. But you cannot have this material. It has never been printed. You know very well it has never been printed. *How do you know it is in the Adams Papers?*"

I told Mr. Adams I did not know, but that I had studied his ancestor for a long time, and such studies permitted one to infer that John Adams might have mentioned these matters in his *Autobiography*. I said that inference was the business of a biographer.

Mr. Adams's voice rose to a pitch of real distress. "Mrs. Bowen," he said, "I wish I had never laid *eyes* on you."

Something in the desperate pronunciation of the noun softened me; plainly, Mr. Adams's suffering was worse than mine. I gave up and we parted in a mutual rush. Downstairs in the little retiring room I threw myself on the couch; the sound of my voice still rang in my ears. The entire Historical Society had been apprised of my work, hopes, ambitions; right now I desired nothing so much as dignified anonymity. A Japanese girl was standing by the mirror, arranging her hair. "Excuse me," she said, "but are you writing a life of John Adams?"

I told the young woman she must know that, by now. Everyone in the building must know it.

She smiled politely, but her next words startled me. "What was the old gentleman afraid of?" she said.

I went home to Philadelphia and fidgeted. How could I complete my chapter without that material? I was genuinely worried, in a condition of frustration, and I could not proceed. At the end of three weeks, on the day before Christmas, an envelope came in the mail, postmarked Boston. Inside, typed laboriously by Mr. Adams, was everything I had asked for. Plainly, he had entered that sacred room, had found what I wanted, taken it down, and copied it line for line. What alchemy melted his New England heart I do not know. I know only that a surge of relief and joy came over me; I can feel it now, some ten years afterward.

Since those hazardous days, matters have begun to run smoothly for me in libraries. Confronted by fifty thousand books I have not lost my diffidence; perhaps it has increased. But I am not at all abashed in the presence of librarians. I can remember the day the tide began to turn. It was in the Pennsylvania Historical Society, at Thirteenth and Locust Streets, in Philadelphia. I was three-quarters through my life of John Adams and needed some eighteenth-century broadsides to brighten my chapters on the Continental Congress. Research for my preceding book, on Justice Holmes, had been done in Boston and Washington; I was unfamiliar with the Pennsylvania Historical Society and no one there knew me. I walked into the building and upstairs to the library, signed my name in the ledger and went to the card catalogues by the window.

I had not gone through the A's when I felt a tap on my shoulder, and the librarian from the desk handed me a folded slip of paper. It was a note from the director, Richard Norris Williams. "Mrs. Bowen," it said, "would you like a quiet room to work in upstairs?"

I kept that message tacked above my desk for weeks. It cheered me, though I had not accepted Dr. Williams's kind offer because I like the genial commotion of the card catalogue room, the companionship of other readers and the nearness of the books. In research libraries, one hesitancy remained, however, to plague me. It was brought on by the repeated question, put to me first by Mr. Elkins on the seventh floor of the Widener Library: "You don't want *printed* material, do you?" That query, always phrased negatively by research librarians, still had power to put me down. Yet even this bogy was shortly due for exorcism. Again, I recall the day.

Because he is hunting for detail, the biographer finds his material, as I have said, in unlikely places, and this is true in libraries as well as in personal interviews or an out-of-door search conducted through the subject's home county or locale. Suppose one wants to find who was proprietor of a certain Philadelphia tavern, favored by John Adams in a hot July of 1775. The matter may be concealed in some quite ordinary volume, say the published memoirs of a cousin thrice removed, or in scattered notes on Philadelphia streets, compiled in the mid-nineteenth century by some finicky antiquarian and printed obscurely at his own expense.

A list of such publications is not impressive to scholars, accustomed as they are to primary or manuscript sources, and I was conscious of it. The incident that liberated me took place in the Free Library of Philadelphia. It began on that vast second floor, where I had gone to check my book numbers, carrying in my hand a list of just such titles as I have described — thirteen of them, each referring to material vital to my subject and discovered by me at the cost of much time and digging.

I had never used this public library, but the general reference collection is large and it seemed likely the volumes would be here, rather than in a more specialized collection. I found my numbers in the cards and took them to the librarian at the circulation desk. "Only two books at a time . . ." she began.

Two blades of grass to a cow, I told myself, would be as nourishing. I left my books on the desk and wandered off. In libraries it is not well to hurry. To the research worker, haste is fatal. The books have been where they are for a long time; they reveal themselves slowly, at their own pace.

Drifting downstairs in search of help, I came upon a door marked *Assistant Librarian in Charge of Research*. For a public library it was an odd, inviting title. I knocked and walked into a big square room, littered from floor almost to ceiling with the tools of the working scholar: bibliographies, dictionaries, encyclopedias, rare book catalogues, and unanswered letters, no doubt from other librarians.

A young man with startling white hair rose from a table where he was writing. I told him my name and what had occurred upstairs. He seized my hand and wrung it, said I could have anything I wanted in the library, took my list, ran an eye over it, and remarked, all in one loud welcoming breath, "Trash! Everything on this list is trash. My name is John Powell. What do you want with third-rate books like these?" — and was on the intercom telephone to start the wheels rolling.

It was the beginning of a lasting friendship. With this young man I could defend myself, and did. How dared a librarian condemn the contents of books he had not read! — I demanded vigorously. These volumes contained letters printed nowhere else, notes from John Adams's daughter to her mother: "I have dined at General Knox's; the General is not half so fat as he was." John Powell was himself a biographer; when the books came he looked into them and made handsome retraction, adding that there is indeed no material the biographer can afford to ignore, whether primary, tertiary or quinquagintal.

History withholds so much! Thomas Carlyle has said it with his usual violence and the hammering of his bold Germanic capitalizations. "Listening from a distance of Two Centuries, across the Death-chasms and the howling kingdoms of Decay, it is not easy to catch everything."

To catch everything? It is not easy to catch anything at all, or at least anything that will communicate in living terms across the centuries. The biographer is much in the position of a journalist who looks for news. Not for fillers or musty historical chestnuts that can be found in the textbooks, but for *biographical news*. Sometimes the biographer's news is gleaned from the mere titles of books. I well remember the summer morning when first I saw the Holmes family library. The books had recently been moved to the Library of Congress, in Washington, and awaited settlement of Justice Holmes's will before being catalogued and arranged. A young librarian, shirt-sleeved against the heat, took me upstairs in a small staff elevator, led me down a corridor, unlocked a door and beckoned me into a narrow, steel-walled room.

Stored and filed on shelves, tables, chairs, were the accumulated personal libraries of three generations of Holmeses, some six thousand volumes in all. Perhaps half were lawbooks; they filled two rooms; yellow library slips stuck out from the pages. Framed pictures, tied in stacks, lay along the floor and there was a wooden box of china, each piece wrapped in tissue paper. At the door a table held a pile of dime thrillers in paper back, with lurid drama depicted on the covers; I wondered if they belonged here and which of the family had collected them.

Altogether it was an inspiring, dazzling, dusty sight. Here were books beloved of Wendells, Olivers, Jacksons, Holmeses, inscribed on flyleaves by donors and owners: "O. W. H. Jr., from his loving father and mother, Christmas, 1859." Here were Dr. Holmes's books on music, acquired no doubt when he was learning to play the violin in the 1850's. (A trying time for the family; the good Doctor considered fiddle playing to be a mere matter of time and application.) I noted the German edition of his *Autocrat of the Breakfast Table* . . . *Der Tisch-despot*. What a travesty of a title, and how had the Doctor felt when first he saw it?

Here were books I had myself been reared on: *The Dolly Dialogues,* Anstey's *Tinted Venus,* the many volumes of old Isaac D'Israeli's *Curiosities of Literature.* There were enough Latin books to stock a school — Mr. Epes Sargent Dixwell's own school, no doubt, where O. W. Holmes, Jr., had studied. And here was Mr. Dixwell's *Phaedrus,* with a signed photograph of William Tyndall pasted in, dated 1877. Here also were the *Letters to a Young Physician, Just Entering upon Practice,* by James Jackson, M.D., L.L.D. That would be Justice Holmes's grandfather, I thought, through the maternal line; he had dedicated his book to that excellent physician, Dr. John C. Warren, Professor of Anatomy at Harvard. There was a chapter on "Somnambulism, Animal Magnetism and Insanity"; there was one on "Phthises" which recommended exercise in the open air, particularly horseback riding. The chapter "On Dyspepsy" went direct to the point: "I believe that very many persons are benefitted from the juice of the grape, and I choose to say so. I love to tell the truth, even when it is unfashionable."

What a very sensible book, I told myself, and copied the sentences in my notes. "On entering the sick room," wrote Dr. Jackson, "the physician's deportment should be calm, sober without solemnity, civil without formality. He should abstain from all levity. He should never attract attention to himself. He should leave the room with an air of cheerfulness. . . ."

During all this time, the librarian had waited, sitting on a box by the door. I paused in my reading to tell him a person could learn more about the Holmeses, here in this little room, than in a dozen interviews with the Justice's friends and relatives. The librarian asked how long I expected to stay. "All day," I said. The librarian replied that he would have to stay with me; readers were not permitted in this room by themselves. I said I was sorry to take up his time. Following my usual procedure I opened my briefcase, took out paper and a dozen sharpened pencils and laid them conveniently by. Then I removed my hat and shoulder bag, produced from the latter a kitchen apron (library dust can begrime one's traveling clothes), and put it on.

The librarian watched. Then he smiled. "I think the library can assume this risk," he said quietly, and took his departure.

I never saw him again. But I remember that young man with gratitude. He led me where I wanted to go and showed me what I had come there to see, then took my measure and left me with the books.

Recently I heard a young lawyer say, "When I go into a really good library, things happen to me." For the librarians there could be no tastier compliment and none more true. Since I began to read in libraries some thirty years ago, times have changed and policies have altered. Modern librarians look on it as their business to make their shelves inviting. A librarian's policy depends, of course, on where he is placed. Among rare books, custodial care is of first importance, whereas in the public libraries of great cities it is important to "get the titles off the shelves," whether or no the volumes fall apart from overwork.

But to the biographer, a scholarly librarian stands at times in the relation of editor. By tactful approach the librarian will discover the scheme of one's book, how widely one plans to explore certain phases of history, certain scenes and personalities. What he says can encourage expansion, a deeper treatment. He calls on the telephone or writes letters at strategic moments: "We are on the trail of that holograph map [or that portrait or manuscript letter]. We have written twice to England and enclose replies to date. We will surely track this item down. By the way, last night our Miss Y. found that 1607 edition of Cowell's *Interpreter*. Do you still want to take it home? . . . May we say your treatment of the Norwich episode is especially valuable and we hope you will not give up but pursue it further."

In the five or six years it takes to write a biography, such expert, persistent interest is to the writer like food to the famished. The librarian has gone beyond the path of duty; he believes in one's book and his involvement proves it. For lack of certain material, the biographer may have deleted a telling episode. But the librarian's letter gives the writer heart. He fishes his chapter from the pile, inserts a blank page on which he scribbles, *Librarian X will supply material,* and arranges his narrative accordingly.

As it happens, I am especially dependent on librarians because my scheme of biography requires that I do the entire bulk of reading myself. Contrary to common practice, I do not engage research workers to go to libraries and read for me, or even to search for specific things. Such a helper, no matter how skillfully trained, may miss something on the way, some side picture, name or incident vital to the illumination of my characters. Therefore I prefer to make the journey alone, though it may add years to my task.

I have known librarians over half the world. I think their praises are not often sung, and I am glad to sing them now. Wherever they are, I salute them and wish them joy of their work.

10
The Search for a Subject

For the biographer between books, the search for a subject is by no means confined to working hours. Like love, it goes on all day. No matter what one is doing — making grocery lists, picking dead roses off bushes or boiling the water for tea, the thing is in the back of one's mind, intrusive, questing, at once a blessing and an irritant. The biographer without a subject has little focus to what he does. Round in his mind the wheels whir, out of gear; he hankers after that push upon the lever, the falling of the cogs, the steady forward movement.

Old Isaac D'Israeli, father of the prime minister, wrote a heroic number of biographical works, among them a delightful volume called *The Literary Character, or, The History of Men of Genius*. In it, the author leads off with a paragraph referring to one of his subjects, but which surely described D'Israeli's own pleasure in his literary labors. "Many peculiar advantages," he wrote, "attend the cultivation of one master passion or occupation. In superior minds it is a sovereign that exiles others, and in inferior minds it enfeebles pernicious propensities and imparts the most perfect independence to ourselves. It is observed by a great mathematician, that a geometrician would not be unhappy in a desert."

Without a subject, without this master passion, the world is the biographer's desert; he feels his mind enfeebled and his propensities pernicious indeed. Looking back on five completed biographies, I see that I for one had trouble with every choice of hero, though afterward I held the illusion that it had been easy, fortuitous, that my subjects had simply walked toward me out of history, the right hand extended in greeting. But it is not true, and old letters and notebooks record my struggle, the doubts and trials, the subjects chosen and worked over for six weeks or six months in all good faith and hope, and then abandoned.

Sometimes the trial period lasted more than a year before disillusionment set in — not disillusionment with the subject himself, but a realization that this man was not for me. There lacked an affinity between us; my study had given me no bias, no point of view strong enough to propel me into a five or six years' journey in time and place, alone but for the company of this man and his associates. Of all my subjects, only the first, Tchaikovsky, came to me not out of history and the reading of books but by circumstance or luck. Barbara von Meck turned up in New York with Tchaikovsky's letters, I read them and was at once enchanted. Even so, the publisher asked only that the letters be annotated and edited; it was after some months of study that I begged an extension of time and wrote a biography.

In that very successful biography, *The Young Melbourne,* one recognizes that Cecil's choice of subject was half his literary battle. Subject and author here are never dislocated but interweave as naturally as the ten fingers of a man's hands, locked one into the other. It has taken me years to learn it, but there are persons of exemplary and even interesting lives, who simply cannot be written about. They do not give themselves to dramatization; they will not emerge upon the stage but linger in the wings, their eyes cast down, refusing to "project." Many women of history are in this category. The virtuous ones, in particular, take their stand in the background, behind the shoulder of a man they have loved or married, a celebrated son whom they have reared. Abigail Adams is a case in point. Begin to write about her and at once her husband, President John, or her son, President John Quincy, steps out and throws his shadow.

Sometimes a subject is chosen because the biographer is interested in a whole category of men. My first two heroes were musicians, for the simple reason that my early training was in music; the musical personality had always fascinated me and I wished to study it. I observed the current crop of performers and composers, I read everything I could find on artistic genius, from Santayana to the Iowa University studies on musical talent. These last, undertaken some twenty-five years ago, confidently divided musical talent into five ingredients. I remember them well: digital dexterity, sense of pitch, sense of rhythm, musical memory, and, surprisingly, love of music. The classification touched me closely because, after years of serious practice on the violin, I recognized that of the five ingredients I possessed just one — the last, which had served me surprisingly.

Certain categories of men and women, like certain individuals, refuse to be written about in full. There are types

that never mature; I think it was Walter Bagehot who remarked that a Cavalier is always young. I could not write
about a Cavalier because I love old men, with their magnificence and their ferocity; to write about Justice Holmes, at
eighty and at ninety, was a joy and an inspiration. Even if,
for lack of space, I am obliged to end the story fifty years
before my hero's death, as in *John Adams and the American
Revolution* — even then I have the sense of my subject's even-
tual old age, of a fruitfulness and ripening before the hero is
cut down. I am possessed by the belief that a man's youth and
early character are influenced by what his old age will be. If
Keats, for instance, had lived to eighty, would he, in youth,
have been less like Keats and more like Wordsworth? It is a
perverse way of thinking; perhaps I am only saying that a biographer must keep in mind the whole of her subject's life, even
while composing that first chapter, "Youth and Education."

The biographer in between books is doubly vulnerable
because biography seems to be everybody's business. For
the novelist, the plot of his next book is a private matter
between himself and his typewriter — a happy secrecy, per-
mitting conception without interference of seduction or extra-
curricular rape. With me at least, my last work is no sooner
on the stands than letters come, suggesting a subject. The
grandmothers of strangers are crying from the grave, it
seems, for literary recognition; it is bewildering, the number
of salty grandfathers, aunts and uncles that languish unappre-
ciated. Telegrams propose a day and hour of appointment,
when I can have the privilege of learning the circumstances
and (irresistible) character of the deceased. Sometimes the
subject is not decently dead but signs the telegram, in which

case wires must be dispatched, stating regret and my plans for immediate departure to far places. Subjects have been known to ring my doorbell, unannounced, and standing upon the mat, all in the open air begin what salesmen call their pitch.

Rival publishers send tactful letters. (How gratified one would have been to receive them, twenty years ago!) If my publisher has not already made the suggestion, their own list could profitably include a biography of George Washington, Jane Addams, Edna Millay, Justice Brandeis, John Marshall, Roger Taney, Clara Schumann or old Judge Sewall of Massachusetts who sentenced the witches and repented. My own publisher, however, is not sleeping. He telephones from Boston with two suggestions, which he refers to as "ideas." Two beauties, he says cheerfully. What is the matter, don't I even want to hear the names?

I do not, and it is best to say so. The fact is that suggested subjects can be dangerous for the biographer, especially if they are forced and pushed, with rewards offered. Some literary forms do not lend themselves to commission-writing; the product emerges tasting of the shop, like fruits laid on, a hothouse breed, lacking the tang and scent of the native product. It is my contention (and it is not original) that an author's books, no matter what his professed subject, are actually about the author. It does not follow that the product is egotistical; Boswell bore little likeness to Samuel Johnson. Yet, whatever form the writer chooses — fiction, poetry, biography — his books are written because he has something to discharge, some ghost within that struggles for release. In company with other writers, I am often asked if I am "with book," or when I expect to "give birth." There is reason for this tired witticism;

in his book an author actually is discharging some part of himself. Could one imagine Carlyle's *French Revolution* being conceived, as subject, by anyone but the author — Froude's *History of the Reign of Queen Elizabeth,* Parkman's *Oregon Trail,* De Voto's *Across the Wide Missouri?* The very titles bear their author's stamp. Here, nothing is machine-made. It is all done by hand, as we used to say of good millinery; its very faults are the craftsman's and convey his message. These books proceed unevenly, like human beings, one moment prosy, the next moment dramatic. They are marked, in short, by that quality which beyond all qualities is difficult for the artist to achieve and impossible to counterfeit, the quality of life itself.

The novelist finds his subject, I take it, in his own experience of living; he looks back upon himself and draws upon his past. The biographer too, interpreting his subject, draws from his past. Could a man who had not known envy write about Sir Francis Bacon, about Florence Nightingale if he had not been driven by a passion for achievement, about Proust if he had never felt neurotic fear? Yet the historical biographer cannot, like the novelist, find his subject in daily life; he takes his subject from books. Biography, like history, is a matter of accretion; its architecture grows from given materials. The biographer is a natural born reader who lives surrounded by bound volumes and draws therefrom his sustenance. Print is his habitat, he swims in it like a fish in a river. This is not to say that the biographer's talent is derivative, less original or less "creative" than the novelist's. I am suspicious of that word, creative. If art has a purpose, it is to interpret life, reproduce it in fresh visions. Filtered through the blood lines of the artist, experience takes on meaning that can be communicated. And the process is as important — and as difficult — whether the reproduction is inspired by the immediate present or by the remote past.

But because historical biographies stem from reading and nothing but reading, the biographer's choice of subject must be defined as recognition rather than conception. This subject existed, this man once lived; the circumstances of his career are to be found in records, letters, deeds, wills, diaries, newspapers, books and all the paraphernalia of scholarship. I had almost said the suffocating paraphernalia; on emergence, I often wonder if my written narrative will survive this crushing bulk, this choking accumulation of library dust. The biographer must be at pains therefore to choose a subject who can survive, whose vitality will penetrate beyond the dreary cerements of death, history and professional scholarship. There have been in the world men and women who seem actually enhanced by death and distance, as if the centuries gave them brighter distinction, a glow and grace not attainable by living mortals or by the newly departed. Sir Walter Ralegh, for instance. One sees him always in motion, striding the London streets, diamonds flashing in his ears, and for all his courtiership an air of the sea about him, of plain sailors and hard work. In our own history, Tom Paine, the pamphleteer, busy at rebellion, debt-ridden, inspired, eternally troublesome to the respectable.

All during the reading for a biography, subjects for future books suggest themselves, stepping from the records with a brave refusal to rest quietly in their past. In my experience these are apt to be engaging personalities, handsome men, busy in doubtful enterprises. It is hard to resist them; their speech is witty and their manners invite. Sin is more dramatic, certainly, than a state of innocence or stubborn virtue.

Yet one does resist. Mere attraction, charm, gallantry, is not enough to sustain so protracted an intimacy. Between biographer and subject there must indeed be recognition, that leap of the blood which signifies affinity. Confronted with his true subject, the writer feels at once the sting and promise of an intimacy to be achieved, provided he has wit and persistence to endure. Between the biographer and fulfillment there stand — he knows it from experience — the proverbial seven trials of strength that fate demands before the lover is deemed worthy. And concerning wicked men, the charming and evil, were their lives, after all, as exciting as legend has it? Would these dark careers hold up, through the years of writing and reflection, and is it possible there is something soft, here, something that gives way when it should resist?

By evil men, I do not mean those who were merely self-indulgent or a trifle perverse in their habits. Tchaikovsky was a homosexual; after *Beloved Friend* appeared, I think every deviate in the state of Pennsylvania looked on me as his champion; they came and told me their hearts until I was altogether surfeited. But Tchaikovsky was first of all an artist, who did not let love or terror block his work. In mortal fear of exposure, tortured by a marriage undertaken to silence scandal, Tchaikovsky put all fear and all torment of frustration into his art. Whether or not his symphonies are to one's taste, no orchestral music ever gave back more intimately the image of the composer. In such a man the struggle assumed heroic proportions. Inexhaustible musical talent on the one hand, unremitting temptation and fear on the other, and over all the courage to surmount — this was "plot" enough for any biographer.

Tchaikovsky . . . the Rubinsteins . . . Holmes . . . John
Adams. Between the completion of one biography and the
beginning of another, very little time had intervened — a week
or two, a month or two. But after *John Adams and the
American Revolution,* a year and a half elapsed before I could
decide on a subject. In my workbook the pages filled rapidly,
arguing pro and con. Four subjects were listed, one below
the other, four possible heroes, with a question mark after
each name:

> *(Coke)?*
> *Milton?*
> *Cromwell?*
> *I. Newton?*

I cannot remember, at this far date, why Coke was put
into parentheses, though his name came first. Queen Elizabeth's Attorney General, Chief Justice of England under
James I, Coke was a politician and Parliament man all his
life; his legal writing informed and harassed the law students
of England and America for nearly three centuries. John
Adams had introduced me to Lord Coke in Adams's own
legal apprenticeship, when he studied *Coke-upon-Littleton*
in Worcester, Massachusetts, with Mr. Attorney Putnam. In
a beautiful edition of Coke's *Institutes* I had seen an engraving
of the old Judge, tall and strong in his robes, his face bearded
below the coif. Face and figure remained in mind, together
with Coke's sayings and courageous actions before a stubborn
Stuart king. Yet the remoteness in time was frightening, not
to mention the mass of legality, the medieval Latin and law
French. Coke's name, moreover, was unknown in America
save to a few lawyers, and this made him a serious publishing

risk; people are slow to buy books about unfamiliar characters of the past.

At this time I had no conscious ambition to approach history by the purely legal path. True, I had written the lives of two lawyers; reviewers called them "legal biographies." Yet the fact that Holmes and Adams were lawyers was for me almost fortuitous. Their careers had touched — perhaps had altered — the course of American intellectual and political history; this drew me to them. But constitutions are not necessarily conceived by lawyers, though lawyers may draft them in the end. Historians have a phrase, "the great curiosity." It has to do only with the past, and as an emotion it is insistent, and burning as jealousy. At the moment, I was restless with it. From Holmes and Adams, each in his century, I had learned that one could not know America, could not discover the foundations of our constitutional government, until one had studied England in the seventeenth and sixteenth centuries. Naturally, I could not continue indefinitely with this backward procession; somewhere a halt must be called. But the story was for me still incomplete, unsolved, there was a hole to be filled.

"Who that sets forth upon a voyage of discovery ever knows whither he may be carried?" It was not a master mariner who said it but old Dr. Jessopp of Norwich, England — clergyman, schoolmaster, historian and reader of books.

11
Trial and Error

The question was, who best could lead me where I wanted to go? What I looked for was nothing less than a perception of the philosophical background that had preceded our significant American year of 1787. Should a lawyer be my guide — a soldier, painter, writer, teacher? Perhaps a poet would be best, a very great poet, whose mind ranged over all aspects of man's life, and who himself had taken a lively interest in his country's politics and legislation. Milton's name I had met often in writing about eighteenth-century New England. John Adams had been only twenty when he noted in his diary: "Friday. Reading Milton. That man's soul, it seems to me, was distended as wide as creation."

Milton had written liberal tracts on divorce and on church government. He had traveled to Florence and talked with Galileo, he had quarreled with Anglican bishops in print and had kept out of the Puritan army only because, as he said, his mind was stronger than his body. Milton wrote on *The Tenure of Kings and Magistrates,* and he published the brave pamphlet *Areopagitica,* defending liberty of conscience and freedom of the press. New England counted Milton among the heroes who had saved Britain from the Star Chamber and the Stuarts; in Boston, *Paradise Lost* was as familiar as the Bible. Just after the local county elections of 1775, Adams wrote from Braintree that the "old rotten rascals" were in power again, meaning the Massachusetts Tories. Up to their former tricks, said John, like Satan and his cohorts after their fall from heaven, "ever to do ill their sole delight." But the quotation, John added, was "perhaps too frolicsome and triumphant for the times."

It was not only Milton's frolicsome poetry but his prose that the American Fathers relied on for inspiration. The colonies, uneasy with repression, moved and jostled for position; Milton's paragraphs seemed written for them: "Methinks I see in my mind a noble and puissant nation rousing herself like a strong man after sleep, and shaking her invincible locks: methinks I see her as an eagle mewing her mighty youth, and kindling her undazzled eyes at the full midday beam."

What a field day for biographical quotation! Milton's lines would carry the book. Moreover, it is good to write about brave men, and this man was brave beyond the imaginations of soldiers. *Her undazzled eyes. . . .* I thought of the passion that underlay the metaphor; could any but a blind man conceive it? What was blindness, and could a seeing person comprehend it? I walked about with my eyes shut, trying to endure the dark; in panic my eyes came open after thirty seconds. To write about a blind man would mean that one must live with the thought of blindness. After five years of intensive reading for Adams, my eyes hurt; they always hurt at the end of a long piece of work. It is not a moment when one favors contemplating what the loss of eyesight would mean. I gave up Milton. If this seems an insubstantial reason, it is to be remembered that a writer lives a biography.

Oliver Cromwell, third on my list, held strong attraction. He seemed to belong with Milton. Thomas Carlyle had coupled the two in a memorable paragraph: "Mr. John Milton, we all lament to know, has fallen blind in the Public Service; lives now in Bird-cage Walk, still doing a little when called upon, bating no jot of heart or hope. Mr. Milton's notion is, That the Protectorate of his Highness Oliver was a thing called for by the Necessities and the everlasting laws . . ."

Like Milton, Cromwell had been a hero of my youth. Brought up by a mother vigorously Protestant, whose father in turn had been a French Huguenot, I was full grown before I could think of the Pope without devil's horns beneath his hat. And was not Cromwell the very George to that old dragon? For a New England Puritan, even the word *bishop* had held sinister overtones. Cromwell would be the very thing; he had put down the bishops as he put down King Charles. One can be swept away by Cromwell; his vitality is a blast of wind. He came into English history, harsh as any purgative, slicing down bureaucracy in despite of little minds. "At the old Parliament," he told the House of Commons disdainfully, in 1657, "I remember well, we were three months and could not get over the word *incumbrances*." On the pages of history the Lord Lieutenant's words resounded; I went about the house repeating them. "It is a very tickle case," says Oliver to the parliamentary delegates, when for the third time they come, asking him to be king.

A tickle case indeed! Cromwell dissolves the Rump and

locks the Parliament House door. Troubled men seek him out. Was it indeed justified, to send away the parliament? "We did not hear a dog bark at their going," says Oliver, and that is all he says. At Bristol, on his return from Ireland, the conqueror is received with a salvo of guns. "What a crowd come out to see your Lordship's triumph!" remarks a courtier. "Yes," says Oliver. "But if it were to see me hanged, How many more would there be!"

One feels the passion in this man; even his humility is passionate. God-intoxicated, indeed, yet marked from his beginnings by an instinctive feeling for his proper place in the world. "I was by birth a gentleman," he tells the Parliament; "living neither in any considerable height, nor yet in obscurity."

Pleasing words and simple, a perfect sentence with which to open a biography. What a pleasure, to describe the genial squire of Huntington, out with hawk and hound along the banks of the river Ouse! It is awe-inspiring to see him hardened, by force of war and circumstance, into the monument that men called Old Ironsides. On the other hand, what a shocking certainty of purpose these self-designated saints possessed, and what unprecedented intimacy with the Deity! The making of laws or the slaughter of the enemy, always they knew it was God's work. "We, after three hours fight, killed and took about 5000. Sir, this is none other but the hand of God, and to Him alone belongs the glory, wherein none are to share with Him." So writes my Lord General, after a battle. And so Saul, in another time, slew his thousands and David his ten thousands, and all to God's private glory and delight.

The Puritan cant, so glib on the pen, no doubt was sincere

in its time. But today one cannot stomach it — not, at least, by the paragraph and page, on and on, interlarding all victories and all distresses. "It's a very vain world," writes Oliver to his friend at the height of fame. "O, how good it is to close with Christ betimes! — there is nothing else worth the looking after. I am not without some assurance that He will enable His poor worm and weak servant to do His will. In this I desire your prayers."

His poor worm? No no, I could not write about the Lord Protector, though I turned from him with regret. "A spleen-struck man," Carlyle calls him. It is delicious to read this Carlyleian discourse; between the editor of *Cromwell's Letters* and the writer of them was extraordinary affinity. "Often thought he was just about to die," writes Carlyle, "and also had fancies about the Town Cross."

What did Oliver see, walking alone, as he passed the Town Cross at dusk? In the shadows, did a figure hang upon it, and was the face, bent down in agony, all too fearfully his own face and countenance? What man of imagination but has seen this vision, at one time or other in his life? And if there was a town cross in Craigenputtock, surely Carlyle, that gloomy descendant of Scotch Covenanters, himself "had fancies"! All great souls, Carlyle says further, have hypochondrias. "Let Oliver take comfort in his dark sorrows and melancholies. The quantity of sorrow he has, does it not mean withal the quantity of *sympathy* he has, the quantity of faculty and victory he yet shall have? Our sorrow is but the inverted image of our nobleness. The depth of our despair measures what capability and height of claim we hope to have."

No biographer of Cromwell could equal the confession,

or make such perfect self-identification with his subject. Reading further into these *Letters,* I was seriously tempted to forget all about Constitutions, change over and write about Carlyle himself. His humors are potent biographical stuff — as instance his *Journal,* under date of 1837. "The Preadamite powers of Chaos are in me and my soul, with excess of stupidity, pusillanimity, tailor melancholy and approaches of mere desperation and dog-madness, is as if blotted out."

Has any man in the world been as gloomy, and as beautifully able to say so? And who but Scottish Thomas could place, before the word desperation, the adjective *mere?* It is really wonderful; one marvels anew at the long-suffering Jane Carlyle, who put up with it. At the height of his creative powers, about to go on a summer holiday and enjoy himself: "I sit," he wrote, "in a sort of mournful, inexpugnable acquiescence, and look at the green and paved world, really not very covetous of anything connected with the one or the other."

To write the biography of such a man would be a venture beyond optimism, into dark regions hitherto, by this biographer, unexplored. A rat, said Carlyle, was gnawing at the pit of his stomach. Yet one has the suspicion that a man so magnificently creative could not have remained melancholy for long; the mere writing down of his dog-madness would have dispersed it. For your born writer, nothing is so healing as the realization that he has come upon the right word.

Milton, Cromwell, Carlyle . . . superb characters, but outside the boundaries of my search. Cromwell's cause is dead; his Great Rebellion ended only by ushering in a second King

Charles. And Carlyle was altogether a literary person; beyond his Protestantism there was little that yoked him philosophically with the New World. Who that went before these men, exemplified the philosophy America fell heir to; or who, at least, had led the Western world to such a philosophy? Not a soldier, surely, but rather a thinker by profession. And how far back must the biographer go in her search — all the way to Descartes, to the French influence that moved Locke and his disciples, to the break with scholasticism and theological absolutism, to the beginnings of the new heavens and the new earth? Galileo's name came to mind and Kepler's, then Voltaire, who explained the laws of nature to man. If what I looked for was a link between medievalism and the modern world, perhaps a scientist should serve as subject? I had often, in years past, thought of writing the life of Charles Darwin. Yet whenever I went back and read his brief *Autobiography,* his *Voyage of the Beagle* and the rest, it seemed that Darwin had written his own story to perfection; there was no use to run after him with pen and paper. Your scientific genius is a species of miracle. Such men do not as a rule develop their minds slowly, through the years, but seem to be born full blown, sprung full armed from godhead. *The Origin of Species,* it is true, was not published until Darwin had reached forty. Yet the idea of it came to him long before. As for Sir Isaac Newton, he said himself that at twenty-three he was "in the prime of my age for invention, and minded Mathematics and Philosophy more than at any time since." These men seem kin and cousin to young champion chess players or those boy geniuses who at sight can square the root of pi.

And where, actually, did the modern age begin? Surely,

with Sir Isaac Newton! The line of inheritance was clear — from Copernicus to Galileo . . . Newton . . . Darwin . . . Einstein. "The incomparable Newton," John Adams had called him. Adams's century indeed came near to deifying Newton; Sir Isaac permeated the century, held it in his hand as he held the pebble in that last peerless statement: "I do not know what I may appear to the world, but to myself I seem to have been only like a boy playing on the seashore, and diverting myself in now and then finding a smoother pebble or a prettier shell than ordinary, whilst the great ocean of truth lay all undiscovered before me."

What a simplicity is in the very great — and the very old! A man who at eighty-odd had made such a statement, could not in his youth be incomprehensible to a layman, a non-mathematician like myself? For years I had been reading, in American Revolutionary pamphlets, about "the Laws of Nature and of Nature's God." To discover at first hand the meaning, one could not stop with Rousseau, but must go farther back to find what our Founding Fathers meant when they tossed those words with so much confidence into their political manifestos. These eighteenth-century statesmen were thinking in terms of what they so proudly called *political arithmetic*. They had in mind a universe newly arranged and systematized. And by this vision the Fathers were vastly comforted. Knowledge of the natural world would set men free. Sir Francis Bacon had hinted at it, Sir Isaac Newton pointed clearly to the way. This universe, which for centuries had been God's secret, Newton probed boldly with his lighted taper. What he found suggested that the system might be no mystery at all but Nature's own arrangement, proven not by Genesis II but by the downward movement of a stone, a feather, an apple. With a prism in his hand, man could explain light itself. God, in short, was reasonable.

"I am going to write about Sir Isaac Newton," I told my publishers. Would they care to draw up a contract?

Their response was cautious. What about physics? they asked. What about optics, and calculus; wouldn't I have trouble with the calculus? Their question seemed beside the point. It was true that at the age of sixteen I had been dropped from school algebra because the teacher said I held back the class. This however had been looked on as the happiest event of my life to date; it banished current intellectual despair and presented me with an extra hour a day to practice on the violin. As for the calculus, a childhood spent on the campus of Lehigh University had taken care of that. Here, each winter after examination week, the sophomores burned Old Man Calculus at night, in a dazzling ceremony known as the Calculus Cremation. My mother did not like to have me go; there was something altogether too realistic in that dark gibbet above the pyre, the stuffed figure swinging, the hooded sophomores dancing around the flames. The ceremony exercised real power. After the figure had been consumed I ran home, convinced that mathematics was done for and finished, without strength in future to harass.

But my publishers, in the year 1950, did not know about the Calculus Cremation. Nor did my husband, whose bent is toward science and who showed satisfaction that I had at last chosen a "worthwhile" subject, meaning a subject who was neither lawyer nor musician. My husband indicated further that he would be happy to help with my scientific education. We had better start with refraction, he said; refraction was the beginning of everything. Procuring a finger bowl of water, he dipped a knife in it, and as the image wavered, he began to explain about refraction. I felt no comprehension but rather a mounting irritation. And what, to a biographer, was this sinister word, *we*: "we had better start." There was no *we* about it, an author writes her book alone. I should have known better than to reveal the subject of a new biography, at least until the thing was past the tentative stage.

I told my husband he had a complicated way of talking, and I fetched the book and read aloud Newton's own description of his youthful studies. *"In the beginning of the year 1666, I procured me a triangular glass prism to try therewith the celebrated phenomena of colours."*

That was the way to talk, anyone could understand it. And besides, I had no intention of stopping long, in this biography, on optics or the calculus, which in Newton's day was not even called calculus — I reminded my husband — but the theory of fluxions. John Adams had studied the theory of fluxions, and he had read Gravesande's *Introduction to Newton,* with which I too was familiar. There were oblique ways of going at things; a biographer need not butt head on into physics. Moreover, I planned to approach matters, not from twentieth-century knowledge but from medieval superstition, by way perhaps of astrology. Astrology after all was half fairy tale, filled with serpents, green lions, flaming suns and poetry. "It was scarce day when all alone" (I quoted) "I saw Hyanthe on her throne. . . ."

Astrology led to chemistry, not physics, my husband said coldly. That depends, I replied, on where one is going when one starts out. What I had in mind was not a book about Newton's scientific discoveries but about his influence on ideas, and hence on the political philosophy of his day and century. From the biographical point of view, Newton was a personality fascinating to contemplate, perhaps the strangest genius of all time, with his concern for Old Testament chronology, his *Observations upon Daniel and the Apocalypse.* I had found lively stories, trivial-seeming, but useful to the biographer. How Newton, at birth, was so small his mother said she could have "put him into a mug," and so low in vitality that two women who were sent to fetch a tonic medicine declared themselves surprised to find the baby still breathing when they returned.

My husband said he would retire from the scene until I got to the calculus, when no doubt I would scream for help. I said maybe, but wasn't it odd, how many great men had sickly childhoods and were driven thereby to reading and contemplation? Newton's schoolboy notebook was helpful, wherein he chid himself for spending money on "china ale, cherries, tart and marmolet." Spent idly and in vain, he wrote sternly, in Latin: *"otiose et frustra expensa."* The little stories were appealing, they brought genius within speaking distance. It was a point in favor, too, that a title for my book had suggested itself: *The Grand Design,* after a line in Descartes' "Discourse on Method." Never before had I found a title until my manuscript was finished and delivered; it seemed a good omen. To an author, his book titles have an active, working significance. *The Grand Design* would cover everything; it would lead my narrative along, give scope.

I talked about Newton everywhere, asked questions, met challenges as they came. It was reckless, I stood in danger of being discouraged by the experts and disheartened altogether. But this was seeking-talk, and necessary. Old Man Calculus, in spite of cremation, came back to haunt at intervals. The president of Swarthmore College, who did not know my educational background, remarked that if "the mere matter of physics" was proving obstructive, I could run over any time and take their freshman course. He could arrange it, he said. I thanked him and withdrew quickly, remarking that I thought I could manage.

In his introduction to *The Garden of Cyrus,* Sir Thomas Browne has a charming sentence of apology. He never was master of any considerable garden, he says, nor would he attempt to write about one, had he not observed "that purblind men have discoursed well of Sight, and those without Issue, excellently of Generation." I read the words and was heartened. Rousseau, too, encouraged with the opening paragraph of his *Social Contract:* "I enter upon my task without proving the importance of the subject. I shall be asked if I am a prince or a legislator, to write on politics. I answer that I am neither, and that is why I do so. If I were a prince or a legislator, I should not waste time in saying what wants doing; I should do it or hold my peace."

And if I were a mathematician, I told myself, I would be busy at the preparation of a monograph on the quantum theory, restricted relativity, or the principle of the excluded middle. I did not plan to write a book on natural philosophy, but the life story of a genius who did.

Thus I rationalized, and thus proceeded with my venture. All in a hurry of eagerness I plunged, splashed, cavorted, swimming ever deeper into waters that would never receive me.

12

A Subject Is Found

The Huntington Library is in San Marino, California, and it is famous among scholars the world over. It has a botanical garden and an art gallery which people come in crowds to see. The library sits in a palace on a hill. An army of Mexican gardeners tends exotic plants, each with its label, stiff and plain. It was March when I was there and the camellias in full bloom A wide *allée* was bordered with double rows of Roman statuary, the figures looking somehow exiled and mournful among the bamboo and palms.

On the face of it, an odd place to come and search for Sir Isaac Newton. I had been reading for some months, I knew about the Huntington collection of eighteenth-century tracts and pamphlets, I was in Los Angeles and had seized the opportunity. On the way to the Coast I had stopped in Chicago to visit two other research libraries, the Newberry and the John Crerar, see what they had and map my voyage further. It seemed difficult to persuade librarians that I was interested in Sir Isaac; nothing in my past performance pointed to an affinity for astronomers. I had become self-conscious and a bit on the defensive. Yet I could not approach the subject lightly. I was deadly serious, more than a little anxious, and besides, where is the light approach to a biography of Sir Isaac Newton?

I wrote ahead to the Huntington, saying that I had only two or three days, and indicating what I hoped to see . . . their first editions of Newton's *Optics,* for instance, and his *Principia.* The Blake drawing of Sir Isaac, bending over a triangle, and naked as Adam. I wanted to see Voltaire's *Elements of Newton's Philosophy,* dedicated to Voltaire's Marquise: *"Minerve de la France, immortelle Émilie, Disciple de Neuton et de la Vérité."* Newton's vogue in France had been enormous; it intrigued me that Voltaire's lady was a propounder of mathematical principles. The Portsmouth Collection had papers pertaining to Newton, with a letter from Newton's mother when he was a boy at Cambridge University.

Of all this I reminded the librarians — the Messrs. Schad and Godfrey Davies — when they met me hospitably at the door. But the flowers? they cried. The famous orchids — didn't I want to see the orchids, first? And the art gallery. The Blue Boy, and Sir Thomas Lawrence's *Pinkie?* Everybody, they said, wanted to see Pinkie.

No, I said; I wanted to see the books. They had, I believed, the earliest biography of Newton, by Fontenelle. "Published in 1728, wasn't it?" I added. (No use mentioning a book to a librarian without its publication date.) Davies grinned. "I see you are going at Newton literary end first," he said. "We have a little schoolbook in the library. Perhaps you know it — published in Philadelphia in 1808 and entitled, *The Newtonian*

System Explained by Tom Telescope. Do you want to see it?"
Of course I wanted to see it. Tom Telescope might clear things up for me considerably. I wanted also to see anything they had about the town of Grantham, in Lincolnshire, where Newton went to school. Microfilm or photostats, whatever they could offer. I told the librarians I had been going over their catalogues. "I have a list of your Newtonia, here in my purse."

In the hallway I stopped and began to dig through my handbag, leaning it against my knee. The librarians laughed, took my arms and propelled me forward. "It is a mistake to be too eager," Godfrey Davies said. "But Mr. Schad will take you to the books.

For three brief blissful days in that March of 1950, I sat at a table in the Rare Book Room of the Huntington Library, while the call-boy brought my volumes. The *Optics,* first. There is no overestimating the value, for the biographer, of handling original manuscript, or the first editions of books written by his subject. I had seen these volumes at home, in later, heavily annotated editions. Here it was not content and matter that I sought but something else, and as the beauiful old books came to hand I lingered, glad that I was alone and could take my time.

The *Optics* opened to an elaborate title page, engraved in red and black. *London, MDCCIV,* it said. In 1704; Newton was fifty. "I have here Published," he had written, "what I think proper to come abroad, wishing it may not be translated into another Language without my Consent. . . . My Design is not to explain the Properties of Light by Hypotheses, but to propose and prove them by Reason and Experiments: In order to which, I shall premise the following Definitions and Axioms."

Not by hypotheses nor the authority of the classics, but by experiment. There it was in all its glory, the statement that had helped to change a world. This was by no means its first expression, but from such a source it was impressive. The casting off of authority and of reasoning a priori had taken many centuries to accomplish, and much bravery of spirit. I thought of Newton's pupil, Gravesande the Hollander, and his book that John Adams had read when he was a student at Harvard College: "Lay aside all feigned hypotheses. The properties of Body cannot be known *a priori;* we must therefore examine Body itself. He only, who in Physics reasons from Phenomena, and pursues this Method inviolably to the best of his Powers, endeavors to follow the footsteps of Sir Isaac Newton, and not he who implicitly follows the opinion of any particular person."

The Huntington had a first edition of Gravesande, the diagrams as clear as if they were drawn yesterday; I paged it over and copied out my quotation, capital letters and all. As for Voltaire's *Éléments de la Philosophie de Neuton,* I fell in love with it at sight. *"Mis à la portée de tout le monde,"* the subtitle said. On the title page, beautifully engraved in two colors, was Voltaire, seated at his writing table, dressed in toga and sandals, and crowned with laurel. Hovering in the clouds above him was Newton with the Globe, and nearby a lady, holding a mirror to Newton, and surrounded by cherubs. The lady, no doubt, was Voltaire's Émilie, *Disciple de Neuton et de la Vérité.* A long, flowery poem in the eighteenth-century manner explained both the lady's virtues and Newton's. How lighthearted, I thought, and how altogether French!

There was something enchanting about it, and about all these books and pamphlets of contemporary comment and exegesis. They made Sir Isaac new and startling; they showed a world that was astounded by his theories. Our own world, in this year of 1950 when I was reading, had recently been astonished in its turn by Einstein's theory of relativity. Only a few months before I came to California, Einstein's formula had been spread one startled morning across the front page of the *New York Times,* scrawled out like the conjuration of a necromancer:

$$E = mc^2$$

People had gone about, repeating it to one another. "Do you understand it, do you know what it means, is it going to *change* everything?"

In my notebook at the Huntington was a charming little poem I had copied somewhere, written long before Newton's day — written, in fact, about 1570, when plain men were still struggling to accept the uncomfortable notion that our earth was round, and that it moved. The poet had apparently pondered the question, and poet-like, had decided it was none of his business except as the discovery brought sadness or joy:

> *Only the earth doth stand forever still.*
> *Her rocks remove not, nor do her mountains*
>   *meete,*
> *(Although some witts, enrich with Learnings*
>   *skill*
> *Say heav'n stands firme, & that the Earth doth*
>   *fleete*
> *And swiftly turneth underneath their feete)*

Yet though the Earth is ever stedfast seene
On her broad breast hath Dauncing ever beene.

Tom Telescope, when I got to him, proved equally light-hearted. "The Newtonian System of Philosophy," said the title page, "Explained by Familiar Objects, in an Entertaining Manner, for the use of Young Ladies and Gentlemen, by Tom Telescope, A.M." Here, set out for youthful eyes, was Mr. Galaxy and Mr. Set Star, the heavens all defined. Opposite page fifty-eight, some young hand, unable to resist, had cut out and kept the picture of "Mr. Blanchard and Mr. Jeffries in their balloon, crossing the English Channel from Dover to France." Here, under "Matter and Motion of the Universe," was Vesuvius, luxuriantly spouting, and here the principle of the mirror, explained pictorially, with images clear, and a fat pointing baby saying, "There Papa, there Mama, there Nurse, there me!" The "elasticity of the air" was memorably illustrated by the tale of one Master Curtis, who fell in the river and was rescued by a passing horseman, who revived him by blowing into his lungs.

It was all very plain and agreeable; it was like *The Stars for Sam,* and if I had been approached thus sensibly in my youth, I would not have met with mathematical disaster at sixteen. Once I got through with Tom Telescope and Voltaire, however, the field darkened. As I picked up the books from my collected pile, I could see that later commentators were not going to be nearly so entertaining. Before tackling them, I sent for first editions of Newton's Biblical studies — *The Chronology of Ancient Kingdoms Amended,* and his *Observations upon the Prophecies of Daniel and the Apocalypse.* They were deliciously bound and printed, attractive in everything but subject matter. How was it possible that Newton had written such books — this genius who adjured the world never to believe what it was told, but to "prove by Reason and Experiment"? The eighteenth century, it was plain, knew how to stretch its own word, *reason,* to include many occasions. "When Manasses set up a carved image in the house of the Lord." So Newton began his argument. To the twentieth-century eye it was purest gibberish; the wonder was that Newton had written it. In every great man, are there these gaps in good sense, these aridities of the mind, dry wilder-nesses where the jackal and the crow pick at the dead bones of superstition? Did Newton turn that extraordinary mind to his Biblical chronologies because he was tired of being de-nounced as an atheist, a man dangerous to religion and piety? There he sat in Jermyn Street with his pleasant niece for housekeeper, tending daily to his business at the Royal Mint and giving his evenings to figuring the proper dimensions of Noah's Ark — this man who before he was twenty-five had changed the basis of the world's thinking.

Could anyone write the biography of such a man? The story would be full of riddles, unsolved queries; it would end indeed on one huge interrogation. I turned to Newton's later commentators, hoping to find a clue. One pamphlet in particular fascinated. It was a lecture, given by a Russian Marxist at an International Congress in 1931. Entitled *The Social and Economic Roots of Newton's Principia,* it outdid in fantasy Newton's *Observations on the Apocalypse.* Great men, said the author, are not great except as they ride on the shoulders of the proletariat. Great men are only the expression of economic forces. I thought of what Newton himself had said of his greatness, giving full credit to those before him —

and not by any means to the proletariat: "If I have seen far-ther, it is by standing on the shoulders of giants."

The Library clock said three in the afternoon. The nadir, life's lowest hour. I looked about me. In the Rare Book Room of the Huntington Library nothing stirred. No fly buzzed in this air-conditioned heaven; the thought occurred that if I remained too long, would I myself catch some contagion of preservation and be found centuries hence among the books, every desiccated inch of me intact? A reader at the next table had gone to sleep, his head fallen forward on his manuscript. He was a thin young man with brown hair; his feet, sprawling outward, showed red woolen socks. A small snore escaped him. At her desk the blonde librarian looked up, then down again to her filing. If the young man had rolled to the floor, I think she would have ignored it. Somewhere a type-writer started up.

Science, said Dr. James Bryant Conant, is a state of mind. I returned to Philadelphia and to my work. As the days wore on, it became plain that Dr. Conant's was a state of mind I never could achieve, though it was not for want of trying. All day I read, and at night laid on my desk sheets of paper with the names of books to read tomorrow. Books to fetch from the library, books to buy, books to write to England for, books I could get only by interlibrary loan. Their very titles repelled: *The Metaphysical Foundations of Modern Physical Science*. What was I doing, wandering in these dark forests of Brobdingnag, lost, blind and rebellious? Each morning when I looked at my desk and the books piled upon it, my gorge rose. I thought of the Earl of Bedford's *Advice to his Sons*: "You are to come to your study as to the table, with a sharp appetite. He that has no stomach to his book will very hardly thrive upon it."

Facts and facts, how I hated them! Massed one upon another, filed and pyramided — these, it seemed, were the whole concern of the scientists. Forever protesting that science was an art, these men turned to facts as if facts gave answer to the riddle of the universe — a notion any poet knows is ridiculous. "I never loved or taught facts if I could help it," said Henry Adams, "having that antipathy to facts which only idiots and philosophers attain."

It was a comfort to think of it; a better historian than Henry Adams would be hard to find. "Some people are unfortunately born scientific." This time it was Walter Bagehot speaking. As I studied, these sayings came to mind and others like them, apt, pungent and for me disturbingly significant. Perhaps I was overreaching, in my desire to learn? Maybe I should narrow the boundaries, fix limits beyond which I should not venture, in this search for Newton. I remembered an incident of my Tchaikovsky biography. Because it was my first biography, I had the illusion that I must know everything, must begin to read at the very foundations of music, as it were. (How, my husband had asked, can you write about a musician if you don't understand the physics of sound, if you don't know the whyfor of overtones and enharmonic changes?) I had put myself through a course of Leibnitz, which nearly alienated me from Peter Ilich altogether. At about this time or later, I met at a party a milk magnate, a tycoon in the milk business, who had assembled a museum of the history of milk. "Where," I asked him, "do you begin, with such a collection? With the whales, the porpoises, the larger mammals?"

"Oh no," he said, easily. "We don't bring the animals into it at all."

Surely there was application here, if I could find it, put my finger on it? With this book on Newton, perhaps I had gone too deep, mapped out for myself too large a geography. Was it Bagehot again, or Sir Frederick Pollock, who remarked of the English people and their extraordinary practical talent for getting things done: "Sometimes it is a gift rather than a defect not to see too far or too wide at once; it may save us from fighting against the gods."

What I should write was a book about Newton without bringing Newton into it at all. The thought came to me gloomily and then, as I pondered it, with more and more pleasure. Reading in the seventeenth century was pure delight — until I came each time to Newton. The seventeenth century meant John Donne, Sir Thomas Browne, John Bunyan, Sir Walter Ralegh. I had been reveling in them one and all; I had spilled over into eighteenth-century England and met with such gems as Defoe's *Journal of the Plague Year,* pertinent because the seventeenth-century biographer needs close acquaintance with the plague. Defoe was chatty, his phrases startlingly of today. "Everybody began to look upon the danger as good and over," he wrote.

I could not have enough of it. I wanted to know what seventeenth-century London looked like, what it ate and above all, what it believed. I had by now, half a dozen thick folders of notes, headed "What They Believed," and divided into sections of time and place. None of these notes, however, had to do with mathematics, optics or specific gravity. Was I to proceed forever, I asked myself, amassing material around my subject, always on the periphery, never coming to center?

Where then was my biographical philosophy of recognition? I remembered Thomas Fuller, in the middle of writing Volume II of his *Worthies of England:* "Pardon, reader," he says, "my postponing of this topic of Statesmen, being necessitated to stay awhile for further information."

For my part it looked as if I were fated to stay indefinitely for further information. There was a horrid indecision in me; I had the sensation that I was running on a treadmill. "This intermediate stage is painful indeed," my workbook declared. "I fight myself all day and at night, fighting first toward, then away from my subject. In the library, surrounded with books, sitting on the floor up in the third floor stacks, I am happy and secure, struck blind with the search, blind I mean to the outside world. But when I get home I realize I have as yet nothing at all, nothing to hold onto."

Indecision began to assume severe proportions, physical symptoms that resembled fright, and interfered with sleep and digestion. I remembered the year before, when I had been visiting in the North Carolina fox-hunting country, and had strolled each afternoon past the stables. One day a Negro groom was brushing a colt, and I paused to watch. The colt was restless, the colored boy's voice slow and beautifully soothing. "Susie," he said, "what cause you got to shake so?"

Had Susie, too, been visited by phantoms of ambition she could not realize; was the coming hunt too wide of her endowments? "The very mind of man, the more it receiveth, the more it loosens and freeth itself. Yet burdens (Gentle Reader) must be fitted to the strength of the bearers." Sir Edward Coke had said it — the lawyer, King James's old Judge, whose name my workbook had relegated to parentheses. The trouble was, my mind had not received, it had only rejected. Why had I kept on so long with Newton, why hadn't I realized that he was not for me? The basic idea had been good; Newton was indeed the symbol of change, of the shift and turn from medieval authoritarianism to the scientific and social empiricism of today. I had been pursuing the proper star but I had been looking at it through a left-handed telescope, running headlong south when I should be facing north.

I let Newton go forever, returned all borrowed library books, set my new-bought ones on a shelf out of reach and felt myself relieved beyond all blessing. I was like a woman risen from a sickbed, or whose ankle had been broken and mended and who could walk again. I turned at once to Sir Edward Coke, with a blitheness of spirit I never could have enjoyed without the long ordeal of Newton. Medieval law, medieval Latin, law French, problems of the conflict of courts — these would be as nothing, compared to the mathematical bog in which I had been dragging. Yet my past year's work would not be lost. I had not confined my reading to the exact dates of Newton's life, or for that matter to Cromwell's or Milton's; my new acquaintance with Stuart kings, with the English Reformation, the Great Rebellion, would be a starting point. Coke's dates were earlier. Yet even the folders on *What They Believed* would come in handy.

Everything, it seemed, came in handy, now that I had truly settled on a subject. The work on Holmes and Adams was like a prelude; without it I could not have attempted Coke's biography and I knew it as I dug into Holdsworth on English Law, and the great Maitland, Usher, Stubbs. Almost at once, a pattern began to evolve; the word *trilogy* came to mind — in publishing circles a word proscribed (book buyers are shy of trilogies). I kept my own counsel here, but I had no doubt that Coke's story belonged with Holmes and Adams. In Coke, as Maitland said, "the common law took flesh." Coke never set foot on American soil, yet his story belongs to the American tradition. Freedom of speech, freedom from arrest in parliamentary assembly, a citizen's right to the writ of habeas corpus, his right against self-crimination under official inquisition — all these, Lord Coke sought for in his time, and we inherited the victory.

I must go to England, I told myself. Not only to see the records; after all, in these days of microfilm and photostat, an Elizabethan biography could be written in Washington and New York. I would cross the ocean in order to feel and sense that country, so near America yet so far away. And I would go by myself; the word "we" must not intrude, however tempting. Exposure must be undergone without protection; a writer cannot stand behind a shield, and there are experiences in which sharing does not mean enhancement but dilution. "You're really going to write about another lawyer?" my husband asked, morosely. He had thought I was coming round to science, he said. Was I quite sure I didn't want to try that freshman course in physics at Swarthmore? The University of Chicago was offering a seminar on Newton's principles: I could take it by mail, the catalogue said.

Glancing at me, my husband burst into laughter. "Don't look like that," he said. "You've settled on your man. Now go to England. Find him, and bring him home in a basket."

13

London and Sir Edward Coke

London is most sweetely scituate upon the Thames, served with all kind of necessaries most commodiouslie. The aire is healthfull, it is populous, rich and beautifull; be it also faithfull, loving and faithfull.

— JOHN NORDEN

Fleet Street, the Old Bailey, the Tower and the Thames, St. James Palace by its Green Park . . . Holborn, Piccadilly, St. John's Wood — names like the word-sounds in a dream, a nursery rhyme. But they are not stale, they have not lost their magic. For the historian there is no end to London. Huge, sprawling, dark, enchanting, its roots go down to the buried stones of Roman walls, to Norman crypts below the pavement. The historian in London is a man possessed; he can lose his soul or find it every day.

Nine million people, within and without the city limits. Driving from the airport in my taxi, through implacable miles of identical brick suburban houses, I was struck with awe. In all this smoky vastness, where would I come upon the living memory of Lord Coke — dead, this summer of 1951, just three hundred and seventeen years? I had not been in England since I was young; the letters I carried were addressed to strangers and had all to do with work, research and history. I had only ten weeks to spend, on this first visit. In that mere scrap of time I must discover if British libraries held enough direct, personal, authentic source material to build a biography; and I must follow Coke around England, examine, if I could, every house and place wherein and whereon he had set his foot.

But an itinerary is no more than a map, a telephone book of numbers to cling to in an alien city. Beneath and beyond itinerary, I wanted to find if this English world were really alien to me, an American. Through his work in the law, Lord Coke belonged by tradition to my country as well as to England; legal scholars have said that Coke "achieved dual nationality." For a biographer there was prime importance in the concept. According to the records, Sir Edward never traveled beyond England, did not invest his money in new-discovered territory and may well have looked on America as a land of painted savages and lost endeavor. Yet if, in London, I should set out to look for Sir Edward as an alien stranger, I knew that I would never come upon him, never see him close. I must find some foothold, not only in the past but in the English present.

It was a hazy notion but not a sentimental one. In Coke the "common law took flesh." I had not written John Adams's story and Justice Holmes's without learning that a people's ethos is made evident in their laws as in their religion. Lord Coke had fought with passion for rules by which we live today. As Chief Justice of the King's Bench and in the House of Commons, Sir Edward had spoken words that had moved me when first I read them and that moved me still. *"It is against law that men should be committed to prison and no cause shown . . . No man shall be examined upon secret thoughts of his heart or of his secret opinion."*

Lord Coke's biography should be, in the end, far more than the narrative of one man's life. Comprehending in time the end of medievalism and the beginning of today, the story was an epic, an Odyssey whose Ulysses, wearing the judge's scarlet, made boundless journeys within the confines of law court and Parliament. Moreover, this would not be the history of a "good man," as good men are counted. Coke was ambitious; his life was set in turbulent times, among men and women whose desire was for power and who reached for it with the ruthless strength of their several natures . . . Queen Elizabeth, Sir Walter Ralegh, Lord Essex and Sir Francis Bacon; Guy Fawkes; Richard Topcliffe who kept the torture chamber in the Tower; Lady Hatton, beautiful and willful; Lord Treasurer Burghley with his spade beard and his gout, his army of private "intelligencers" and his clever, patient, crookbacked son, Sir Robert Cecil.

Born under Mary Tudor, before he died Coke had experienced four sovereigns; in his last Parliament, Coke sat with Oliver Cromwell. In all of recorded history, no era offers a more varied, crowded and exciting scene. Colonies found and lost beyond the ocean; the Protestant religion established after bloody conflict . . . queens beheaded on the block, and martyrs burned for their belief. Plain men coming to know their rights, the House of Commons rising to its level. . . .

> *With many shocks that come and go,*
> *With agonies, with energies,*
> *With overthrowings and with cries,*
> *And undulations to and fro —*

So Coke's world pursued and resisted its destiny. In Sir Edward's boyhood the very world was shorn of its four corners and said to roll in space beyond old Ptolemy's circles. Sensible men resisted the idea. (And if the earth forever turns — where then, asked Dr. Recorde in his book, shall quietness be found?)

It was an Iliad, this story. Bumping and sliding on the seat of my airport taxi, I heard the afternoon traffic roar up Piccadilly as we neared Brown's Hotel. With my fingers crossed I drew a long breath, praying for good hunting and a biographer's luck.

"No readers allowed under 21," the official folder said, *"nor will the recommendations of lodging house keepers be accepted."*

The Manuscript Room in the British Museum is indeed no place for babes and children. The building is enormous, the main Reading Room has seats for five hundred readers. I got lost not once but three times. In the George III Collection the policeman joshed me. "You need a guide, don't you, madam?" The trouble was that I came in the back door. Having daily morning business at the University of London, it was my habit, on leaving the University, to cross Montague Place and enter the Museum from the north. The first time I got lost I was looking for the print room on the top floor. I wanted pictures of Coke's London, contemporary

prints that would show me old London Bridge, Greenwich
Palace, the Tower, the ships at Deptford yards, the Temple
Stairs and the Thames as Coke knew it. An infinite climbing
of marble steps landed me repeatedly in a gallery of glass
cases filled with the relics of Ur and Babylon; I went down
to floor level and began again. "Entering the British Museum
to find a sixteenth-century print," I wrote home in desperation, "is like entering the seventh level of hell to find a
strawberry."

The Manuscript Room, when one finds it, is tucked away
somewhere behind the main Reading Room. And it, too, is
no place for loiterers. Merely to learn the research procedure
is confusing, and one cannot keep running to the desk with
queries. Figuring out the call numbers in four Harleian
folders, I wasted thirty minutes before I discovered that plain
6687c was sufficient for the manuscript I wanted to see. The
custodians of the manuscripts are scholars, and wonderfully
polite. One of them, bringing me a book, whispered that the
"gentleman across the table is an American, too — Keeper of
Drawings at Princeton University."

What a pleasant title, I thought, and had the Princeton
scholar made it up, as the simplest way to explain himself?
In England they call librarians *Keepers,* as if the building
were a zoo. Mr. Oldman, Keeper of Printed Books, showed
me Coke's own copy of Judge Littleton's *Tenures,* with
Coke's scrawled marginal notes, showed me also the famous
copy of Francis Bacon's *Novum Organum* which Bacon had
presented to Sir Edward. It was a large beautiful white
vellum volume, gold-tooled and stamped with the Bacon
family crest, a golden boar. Lord Coke hated Bacon. On the
title page Coke had scrawled, in inky Latin, *Gift from the*

author, and under it an angry couplet, destined to be quoted down the centuries:

> *It deserveth not to be read in Schooles*
> *But to be freighted in the ship of Fooles.*

How these great men had loathed each other! A battle of the giants . . . Open rivals for the place of Attorney General and for the hand of Lady Hatton, with Coke the victor on both counts — though London legal wits had laid their bets the other way: "the *Bacon* may be too hard for the *Cook*." From that moment on, I remembered, Bacon had done his best to ruin Coke, and Bacon's best was no mean effort. In the end it had been Bacon's machinations that cost Sir Edward his place as Chief Justice of England . . . And then the last ironic scene in the House of Lords: the great Lord Chancellor Bacon impeached for bribery by the Commons, and condemned, his full confession heard. *"Without fig-leaves, I do ingenuously confess and acknowledge . . ."* Old Coke standing with his colleagues behind the bar, silent as judgment was pronounced.

Was ever enmity so dramatic? The story had all the elements of high tragedy — great men contending, and Bacon, greater of the two, a genius of incomparable intellect, defeated by his own incurable weakness of character. How was I to tell this story, would it run away with my book?

It might be well to see what had been written about Sir Francis Bacon, to date, and all of it. I walked into the circular main Reading Room, big as Grand Central concourse, and made my way to the catalogues, which are not neatly kept in file drawers but in huge old ledgers which one must take from the shelves oneself. I drew out the volume marked *Bacio to Bact,* turned toward my preëmpted desk, tripped over nothing at all and fell flat, clutching the volume. I rolled over, got to my feet and glanced embarrassed at the librarians in the central cage behind the double barricade of catalogues. They paid no slightest attention to me, likely enough because they saw the catalogue was unharmed. Making my way carefully to my seat I had a momentary prophetic glimpse into the hearts of these impassive gentlemen, busy behind their barricades. Surely their lives must come, in the end, to be altogether divided and mapped by some mystique of alphabet, at the same time helpful and limiting.

In my catalogue under Bacon the first entry was for Lady Ann, the mother of Sir Francis. Wife of Lord Keeper Sir Nicholas Bacon, with his three chins and his rollicking quick wit, Lady Ann was a character in herself, a bluestocking, reader of Greek and Latin, one of three celebrated sisters. The catalogue listed Lady Ann's translation, from the Latin, of Bishop Jewel's *Apologie of the Church of England,* also *Fourteene Sermons, Translated out of Italian.* . . . I recalled the lady's fanatic Protestantism. A hot zealot, she was, next thing to a Puritan and forever harping at her sons on the subject.

After Lady Bacon, the catalogue jumped four centuries to one "Bacon, A., of the Atomic Energy Research Establishment," author of a pamphlet entitled "The Determination of Uranium by High-Precision Spectrophotometry." How fascinated Lord Bacon would have been! — I thought. High-precision-anything would have been meat and drink to that all-embracing Renaissance mind, with its boundless reach. And surely no one in history had written so much, and had himself been the subject of so much print? I turned the big catalogue pages as fast as I could; it would be closing time before I got to C for Coke. Light in the Reading Room came from above, through arched windows in the dome; my page was darkened now and again by passing clouds. . . . *Letters and Remains* . . . *The Advancement of Learning* . . . *The New Atlantis* . . . *Poems* . . . *The Essays,* with the different editions listed. I longed to send for the books and read again the terrible cold wisdom: "Better to be envied than pitied. . . . Always let losers have their words. . . . The cat knows whose lips she licks. . . ."

And here were Bacon's speeches in Parliament, on the *Post-Nati* and the *Case of the Commendams.* Coke had taken the opposite side in both arguments. Here too was Bacon's *Declaration of the Practices and Treasons attempted and committed by Robert Earl of Essex.* A shameful business, with Bacon standing to betray his friend in open court, then betray him again by printed pamphlet — and all to please a monarch and gain favor. How could so great a genius be so small of heart? The elemental serpent was in this man. "He had," wrote Aubrey, "a delicate, lively, hazel eye; Dr. Harvey told me it was like the eye of a viper."

Not a pleasant character, Lord Bacon. Yet I told myself that I would give all I possessed to see him, and to hear him talk. "A rare man," said a contemporary, "I think the eloquentest that was born in this isle." Could any biographer write about Lord Coke and not be led aside, seduced altogether by the Bacons and Raleghs and Elizabeths? The biographies of Bacon went down the catalogue page, from Abbott to Montague to Spedding. The German commentators came next, with their heavy solemnity of scholarship. Bacon, *seine Stellung in der Geschichte der Philosophie* . . . Horrors! Must one look into *that?* Bacon would have laughed at the title — or would his ever-sensitive vanity have responded? At the last, comprising a good third of the catalogue, was a listing of "Baconians," ready to die for their conviction that Bacon was the author of the "so-called Shakespeare plays." Bacon was actually, I read, the son of Elizabeth and the Earl of Leicester. . . . He wore a magic ring. . . .

I tore myself away. I had no time for nonsense, however intriguing. The first closing bell was ringing in the Reading Room. Four o'clock, only half an hour left. Already I had carried my slips to the desk for volumes needed tomorrow; the books would be ready and waiting next morning. Yet I knew that I must limit this reading and this delightful digging among catalogues and Harleian folders. The days were passing; in these brief weeks I could do no more than survey the field, looking to return. Moreover, the legal bookshops of Chancery Lane had treasures they were willing to part with. Already I had acquired many volumes; there was no doubt but I could do the greater part of my law study at home. The jurisdiction of courts, Coke's long fight with Chancery, comparative procedure in the criminal courts of the Continent, the Commons' battle against the prerogative — all this was available on my side of the ocean. In London I had even met British scholars who planned to spend a year in Washington, studying sixteenth-century England at the Folger Shakespeare Library.

In the Museum the bell rang again. Half past four. I walked out to the pillared portico, where pigeons strutted and complained, thence down long steps to Great Russell Street and the City.

I went up and down the Thames in water buses, looking for Coke's London. In Sir Edward's day the Thames had been London's highway, the Strand being no more than muddy track until Sir Robert Cecil paved it half a mile for his convenience. Today the waterside is dingy and industrial, where in Coke's time it was green and beautiful, lined with walled mansions down to Westminster. In spring the salmon came upstream, fat and sweet. Nevertheless the river is still at the heart of London; a mile inland one feels its presence and hears, when the wind is right, the hoarse blast of the barge horns.

The old prints and pictures I had seen in the Museum were vivid and down to earth; they had shown the sailors' wash flutter from the rigging of a galleon tied by the Tower wall, and small craft foundering in the current that ran between the stanchions of London Bridge. Today the Bridge is easily passed and the galleons all are Diesel. Yet here on the river I felt the past more keenly, I think, than anywhere in London. The little pleasure boat that I rode moved busily with the tide. Mothers and their young children crowded on the deck, young men sat close to their sweethearts by the railing. On the water the royal swans sailed by, black with oil and silt; once a year the keepers wash them. In Coke's day they must have been white as milk, nobody could catch and eat them but majesty.

For a shilling I acquired a booklet called a Water Guide, with maps giving the names of the ancient landing stages: Billingsgate, Ebbgate, Queenhithe, Blackfriars, Temple Stairs. How well I knew the names! Here was the Inner Temple, where Coke had studied law and where he lived in chambers when his beautiful young second wife, Lady Hatton, made home uninhabitable. The Temple Gardens are long and quiet above the Embankment, the lawyers still walk in pairs by the rose borders, carrying their green bags. West of Temple Stairs, Essex House once had risen behind its walls. Here the Earl's plotting friends had met, coming down river by night and leaving their boats at the landing — young men, ambitious, altogether foolhardy, planning to depose a queen yet not knowing really what it was they plotted. I think a handsomer man than Essex never lived, with his melting eyes and easy strong shoulders, the light hand laid on the jeweled sword hilt, all too ready to draw in anger. Thus the painters showed him, "so deeply strook with the harping-irons of malice," a contemporary said. The queen had loved Essex, scolded him, boxed his ears when he was insolent, imprisoned him, pardoned him — and cut off his head.

Sir Edward Coke had been principal prosecutor at the trial of the Earl, in Westminster Hall. Here was the greatest lord in England. But Attorney General Coke, standing in his black woolen gown, had exposed him before that vast audience without benefit of courtesy. And in truth the man was dangerous; Elizabeth could have lost her throne to Essex. Her cousin, Mary of Scotland, had forfeited a crown for love; Elizabeth's judgment against her own lover was a measure of her courage, of her good sense and of her first loyalty, which was to England. I never thought of it without pride. "She is only a woman," said the Pope, her enemy, "only mistress of half an island, and yet she makes herself feared by Spain, by France, by the Empire, by all. . . ." "The choicest artist in kingcraft," said an English subject, "that ever handled the sceptre in this northern climate." "By God, this queen is extremely wise," said a Continental visitor, "and her eyes are terrible."

It was wonderful to know that Coke had entertained Queen Elizabeth at his country house, when she went on progress with her train. Coke gave her, on that summer day of visitation, jewels "to the value of over one thousand pounds." I thought of it as we passed the site of Essex House. On my water bus a young man was playing an accordion; two girls got up and began to dance. . . . Here on the riverbank, Somerset House had stood, and there the enchanting walls and turrets of Durham House, where Sir Walter Ralegh enjoyed his heyday before disaster struck, and where he wrote and pondered in his high study chamber; "a little turret," wrote Aubrey, "that looked into and over the Thames, and had the prospect which is pleasant perhaps as any in the world, and which not only refreshes the eye-sight but cheeres the spirits and (to speake my mind) I beleeve enlarges an ingenious man's thoughts." Ralegh had kept a stable of forty horses at Durham House. The stampings and neighings, the shouts and laughter of grooms and men-at-arms must have echoed cheerfully across the water.

Sir Edward Coke as Attorney General had not only prosecuted Essex, but as King James's Attorney he had been principal prosecutor when Sir Walter Ralegh was tried for treason in the year 1603. A man so accused was allowed no lawyer to defend him; the trial had been a day-long duel between Coke on the courtroom floor and Ralegh, standing in the prisoner's dock. Coke's brutality to Ralegh has long been a byword in legal circles; I had seen it quoted in lawyers' journals at home and abroad: "Thou viper — spider of hell! I will prove thee the rankest traitor in all England." Sir Walter defended himself in an outpouring of purest poetry. Eight months before the trial, Queen Elizabeth had died, an old woman in a red wig. But Ralegh, from the prisoner's dock, never spoke of her as old. "A lady," he said, "whom time had surprised." Guilty or innocent, Sir Walter's words were deeply moving. He spoke of England, of the Spaniard and of sea fighting, in terms that Shakespeare might have used.

What was to be done with such a scene, with Coke's brutality and Ralegh's bravery? "How are you going to get round it?" — the barristers asked me, on Fleet Street. I said I had no intention of getting round it; I would tell the story straight, as the records gave it, and let readers make their own judgment. To me the strangest thing about Ralegh's story was the feeling against him in contemporary England. Sir Walter was loathed, despised; on his way to trial the populace had hurled stones, mud, tobacco pipes at his coach; Sir Walter's jailer said he might have been killed on that journey. Ralegh was contemptuous. "Dogs do ever bark at those they know not," he said.

Was it Ralegh's pride the people hated, his rapid rise to wealth and power under the queen's favor? This plain man of Devon was fabulously rich. In silver armor he stood by the royal door, turning away suppliants with his air of insolent authority. "Damnably proud," said a contemporary. Princes, it is said, have been killed by the populace for their politeness — why not for pride? It was no riddle to understand Ralegh's attraction for Elizabeth. The man's fascination carries down the centuries: the arrogance, the curly beard, the soft voice with the Devon burr, the limitless dark imagination. In the streets his name gave rise to ballads:

Ralegh doth time bestride,
He sits twixt wind and tide,
Yet up hill he cannot ride,
For all his bloody pride.

My academic friends teased me about my predilection for the river. "What are you doing on the Thames in water buses?" they asked. Why didn't they see me in the Public Record Office every morning with the other scholars, going over the State Papers of Elizabeth and James, or the Historical Commision Reports? "I have to know the Thames," I told them. "I have to know it from Greenwich all the way past Deptford where the ships are, and past St. Paul's and the Temple, to Westminster and the Old Palace Yard."

Before I could write about Lord Coke — though I did not say this to the professors — I had to see how the sun struck or slanted behind Westminster Abbey, the parish church of St. Margaret's, and on the water to the eastward below the Tower of London. I had to feel the presence of this river like a native, and its promise of the sea nearby. I myself was raised on tidewater, and like all such persons I am conscious of the wind's direction, the threat or pledge of coming weather. Above the river I noted how the sky looked at different times of day. It is cloudy on the Thames; the wind blows, and after a shower, light strikes through the haze in spears. Americans live out their lives on a continent, a huge solid block of earth. But Sir Edward lived on an island, a small island, and it affected him in his blood and bones as it affects every Englishman, from what he eats and drinks to his governmental foreign policy. I remembered a young Englishman whose business kept him much in the United States. He loved the sun, but it made him at times uneasy. "New York has a hard blue sky," he said. "I miss the clouds; we Englishmen were born in the fog."

Actually, my academic friends were kind to me, in the Public Record Office. They made me familiar with the Historical Commission Reports, the State Papers Domestic and the Calendars of Venetian Papers that contained so much of pertinence and delight. Two celebrated American scholars were reading there, that summer, the Professors Conyers Read and Lawrence Gipson. After work we would go out together and look for something to eat in Fleet Street around the corner, sitting almost silent at the table, our eyes glazed with reading. *"Why* is the P.R.O. so exhausting?" Professor Read asked, one day, taking off his glasses and wiping his eyes. "It is because we have so little time," I said. "In a minute we will all be home again, in Pennsylvania, and we will wish we had worked faster."

The sense of pressure made it like a race. The Round Room at the Public Record Office is the most impressive library I have ever seen. It has places for about sixty scholars; they sit writing at long tables under a skylight. The librarians wear white coats, like hospital internes, and they are quick about their business. In July it was cold in there. I wore wool stockings and wool underwear and two sweaters and a raincoat that I kept on all day, and I never got warm. The Round Room opens at ten in the morning. Fifteen minutes later there is not a seat to be had; I was continually fearful that I would be asked to give up my place to some visiting pundit who outranked me in scholarship and general attainments. From the moment I entered until I left it, the Round Room filled me with awe. I have never known an inhabited place to be so silent. A peculiar crackling sound persisted, small and intermittent, like a mouse at midnight. It came from thirteenth-century parchment, being unrolled slowly, line by line as readers went down the skins.

The material that one can see in the Round Room is quite incredibly valuable. To read there, one has to come with affidavits from one's national embassy — and no wonder. Even to handle these manuscripts is exciting. Coke's biography would, I knew, comprise four great state trials for treason: the trial of Essex, of Ralegh, of the eight Gunpowder Conspirators in 1606 and of the Earl and Countess of Somerset (murder and scandal in high life). In the index to a volume of the Domestic State Papers, I looked up "Ralegh, Sir W." and turned back to the text. Copying out a number I carried it to the desk, and in a few minutes had at hand a thick, leather-bound volume entitled *The Ralegh Book*. In separate sheafs of yellowed manuscript, I read the story as it really happened: *"wie es eigentlich gewesen,"* as old Ranke had said. I saw Sir Walter's handwriting. I saw depositions taken from prisoners, written or signed by Attorney General Coke, with Coke's marginal suggestions, addressed to his legal aides for use in the courtroom — what to recite and what to omit. Terrible suggestions, some of them: *"Read not this."* "This" pertained to King James I, and what it said was not flattering — patently unfit to be read aloud in court, with the royal ear pressed to a listening tube behind the arrased wall.

Did lawyers in 1603, then, leave out whatever was inconvenient to their case, and let the poor prisoner die for lack

of evidence in his favor? Obviously, they did. *Read not this.*
When I came to 1606 and the Gunpowder trials the record
was even more shocking. I saw Guy Fawkes's signature
before and after torture; it needed no expertness in Elizabethan handwriting to recognize the fearful difference. In
his published books, Coke boasted that England, unlike the
Continent, held torture to be illegal; by the common law
there was no authority for it. Yet here I read of Fawkes
tortured on the rack and of Father Gerard, the Jesuit, sus-
pended by manacles to his prison wall, while for three days
they questioned him, and for three days he refused to answer,
fainted, was taken down, and on revival, hung up again.

A diligent searching through Coke's *Institutes* showed
that this torture was ordered by authority of the royal prerogative, not by the common law. Moreover, it was never done
for punishment, after conviction and condemnation, but by
way of questioning a newly caught suspect. It was, in short,
torture by the royal grace, exercised in defense of the realm,
for what men called "reasons of state." That this made it no
easier for the prisoner was a fact overlooked. A "taste of the
rack," a "stretch upon the brake," was considered salutary
when the suspect proved stubborn. Often enough the mere
sight of the rack induced confession. Sitting in the Round
Room, with the evidence at hand, I began to feel sick at my
stomach. The violence of the times was fearful. What had I
jumped into, with this biography of Coke? Was mankind
cruel by nature or did the age demand it, and had I lived all
these years thinking that our Western world was ruled by
law, when actually it was governed by passion, hatred and
fear? Is this what history teaches? Charles Beard once had told
me, "You have to have a strong stomach, lady, to study his-

tory." I thought too of Lord Acton's words: "No priest, accustomed to the confessional, and, a fortiori, no historian, thinks well of human nature."

Amid such violence, how had Sir Edward Coke managed to stay alive for eighty-two years, dying peacefully in his bed at Stoke Poges? Was it an achievement of strength, of luck, of craftiness? It would be my business to find out, through this mine and countermine of plot, treason and betrayal that was Stuart England. I thought of old Lord Treasurer Burghley's code cipher in the 1590's. Three separate armadas, Spain had brought against England in that decade; as the enemy increased, Burghley ranged for code names through the animal kingdom to the zodiac. Father Parsons the Jesuit was *Ferret,* Father Creighton was *Weasel.* The Pope was *Beware,* the Emperor, *Doubt,* and the King of Spain was *Scorpio* . . . "In these queasie and most dangerous times, wherein Truth is manacled by Opinion and Imagination . . ."

So Ralegh wrote from Guiana in 1617. The title to Coke's biography would have to include the word *treason,* it seemed; I might call it *Treason, Sovereignty and the Common Law.* Leaving the Round Room and the Public Record Office, I walked down Chancery Lane, across Fleet Street and down Ram Alley to the Temple Gardens, thence to the Embankment. Sitting on a raised bench with an assortment of friendly characters who smelled of drink, I watched the wide brown river flowing past, the gulls above, the tugs and barges busy. In the afternoon sun it was oddly quiet, the traffic behind me was muted in the wind. . . . Those poor devils in the Tower — Coke had questioned them not by the pair or the dozen but by the hundred. Night and day he was at it. One of his letters to Secretary of State Winwood was dated "From the

Tower, at 3 o'clock in the morning." The nasty thought came to me that Coke enjoyed it.

Was Sir Edward Coke a great man? I would know, I told myself, when my book was done. In history the "great man" formula is elusive. Fashions change. One generation reveres its martyr saints, the next is all for generals of the army. But people tire of generals, they are too stiff. Something homelier is looked for — a Lincoln, with the melancholy furrowed face of wisdom. Once or twice in a thousand years the world accepts a philosopher as hero, but never until he has been safely dead for at least six generations. . . . What was Coke's character? He had left almost no personal letters; the diaries, correspondence and domestic records on which biographers rely were lacking.

Yet the lawbooks that Coke wrote — four volumes of *Institutes,* law reports in thirteen parts — revealed him on every page. Lord Bacon had censured Coke for this; his *Reports,* said Bacon, held too much *de proprio,* too much of himself. It was true, and it was also the biographer's good fortune. Telling a legal tale, Coke's emotions overmaster him and he stops short: "And what heavy event ensued thereupon," he writes, "let historians inform you, for it is grievous to me to remember it." Queen Elizabeth was long dead when the *Institutes* were published, yet Sir Edward remembers her ardently. "Queen Elizabeth," he writes, *"Angliae amor."* And surely no man ever had such passion for the law; Coke spoke of the law as a Sidney, a Drake, a Ralegh spoke of glory and of England. "Methinks, that oftentimes, when I ride by the way, I see the effects of justice rightly resembled, when I behold a river with a silver current . . ." Coke's passion for the law and for scholarship were one and the same, part and parcel of each other. "True it is," he said with his usual candor, "that I have been ever desirous to know much. And do owe more to my profession than all my true and faithfull labours can satisfy."

Not for a moment, in these books of the law, does Coke let the reader doubt where he stands politically. Writing on the jurisdiction of courts, he describes that highest law court of all, the Parliament. "And the parliament holden in the third yeare of our sovereign lord king Charles was *benedictum parliamentum,* the blessed parliament. The severall reasons are yet fresh in memory."

They were indeed, and to all who live today under the tradition of the English common law, they are still fresh in memory. That was the Parliament of 1628, which presented to an angry Charles the celebrated *Petition of Right,* a model for our American Founding Fathers, when they drew up remonstrances to King George III. Coke had been the moving spirit of that petition; he was seventy-six years old at the time.

"But do you like him?" the barristers had asked me, on Fleet Street. "Do you like Lord Coke, that old curmudgeon?" Oh, what did it matter if I liked or hated him? The man had fire in his vitals, and strength and honesty; he was capable of reverence. "Tough old Coke," Carlyle had called him. "Tough and true." But Coke was not always tough, and I knew it. There had been an incident after his marriage; I had come across it in the Round Room. Coke was forty-six when his first wife died — the gentle Bridget Paston who had given him seven sons. In no time at all he married Lady Hatton, aged twenty. She kept her own name. (Why descend, after a position so distinguished, to plain Mistress Coke?) Five months had not gone by when the marriage was doomed, and most of London knew it. Coke, going about his business in his black robe of Attorney, was like a man demented. I had seen the affidavit of one Mary Berham, as of April, 1599: "It is no marvel Mr. Attorney wept, sitting with the Judges, for he has gone up and down ever since his marriage like a dead man, discomforted."

Tough old Coke. A man had need of toughness, who passed his days amid such company. Sitting on my bench above the Thames I paged over my notes in the folder that I carried, thinking of the Tower and the prisoners, thinking of Coke. Was I never to find a word of warmth or affection penned by him, and addressed not to the law but to a human being, someone close to him? "Why do I like him, for I do," my notes read. It was nonsense to think that Coke had enjoyed the suffering of those poor manacled wretches. In his *Institutes* he deplored the harshness of the English criminal procedure. "If there were any spark of grace or charity in a man, it would make his heart to bleed for pity or compassion." Absurd and worse, to judge Lord Coke by the standards of today. A man operates within the framework of his times: it is the cardinal rule of biography, and the hardest to keep. Was that what the professors at home had meant, about *presentism?* If so, I owed them an apology.

Treason! The word and the facts surrounding it might well be the keys to Coke's proverbial harshness. In all the calendar of criminal procedure, no crime is so murky, so mysterious and indefinable; no crime arouses men's passions to such degree. From the day that Coke was born until he died, seven years before Cromwell led England to rebellion, his country was beset by foreign enemies and plagued by traitors at home. Traitors real and fancied — racked, ruined or rewarded by the state — and so-called traitors in religion, who wished to see a Catholic ruler on England's throne. "A toleration of religion," they called it. I remembered the famous "Bloody Question," put to Jesuits at their trials: "Should the Pope send an army to England, for whom would you fight, Rome or England, the Pope or the Queen?"

For a loyal Catholic who was also a loyal Englishman, there could be no answer. Lord Coke himself had put the question, time and again, and had been altogether nonplused by the answers. Jesuits were skilled talkers, and magnificently trained. "Strange opinions of these boy priests and devilish good Fathers!" Coke wrote. And yet — was the Bloody Question any worse than the questions asked in the United States by "investigators" in this summer of Our Lord, 1951? Leaving my place on the Embankment, I walked westward along the Thames; across the water the Parliament Houses came in sight, solid against the sky.

I thought of my countrymen, the Senators. In a panic over Russia and Communism, they had embarked on a witch hunt, day by day condemning the innocent with the guilty . . . Remington sued for perjury, Alger Hiss in prison . . . university teaching staffs dismissed in crowds for refusing to give the names of friends who might be Communist sympathizers . . . plain citizens harassed by summons to take oaths of loyalty — those same oaths to which Coke's compatriots had objected so stoutly. "The thought of man shall not be tried, for the devil himself knoweth not the mind of man." An English judge had said it, long before Coke's time. In Sir Edward's day, the official excuse for such inquisition had been "reason of state." Coke had protested the words angrily, in Parliament. "Reason of state lames

Magna Carta," he said. In America the reasons differed but the operation was equally reckless. After war or revolution, men smell a traitor behind every bush. Senator McCarthy's star was on the rise.

On the printed page the biographer dares not make historical analogies. Yet he perceives them none the less, and they can draw him strongly to his subject. Coke had need of toughness; this much I had learned in London, within doors and without. But how did Sir Edward develop this quality, whence did it come? A man is not born with his fists clenched. Or is he? There was a legend about Coke's birth — how his mother had sat downstairs on that cold February day, warming herself by the fire, when suddenly her body was gripped by pain. Before she could do more than rise from her chair, the boy was born. Long afterward, when Coke was famous, country people thereabouts liked to tell the story. They thought it characteristic — the strong man child leaping onto the hearth without warning, giving out his feeble cry of rage and protest.

Leaning on the parapet and gazing across the water to where the Lords' tower reared its height, I thought it would be well to go to Norfolk, the country of Coke's birth, and see for myself the quiet places that had nourished him.

14

Norfolk, Holkham House and Journey's End

Norfolk, my dear and native country.
Coke, First *Institute*

It is a harsh and windy country, where Coke was born. Sea birds scream above the farms; the fog rolls in from Yarmouth. On the open Wash to the northwestward, seals slide and bask, and along the famous inland waterways sailboats and barges make their way; at nightfall the otter and the badger creep out upon their business on the shores. Three-quarters of Norfolk county is bounded by open ocean; the winds and the whales sport unimpeded down from Greenland. At Cromer on the North Sea, bathers run on the shingle in dark wet winds that only Eskimos or Englishmen would brave. London as the crow flies is not a hundred miles to the south, yet Norfolk is as different from the soft Thames valley as Maine is different from Virginia.

I hired a little car at a Piccadilly agency, set my teeth

against the left-hand traffic and drove out of London by the northeastern route, planning to cross the Suffolk boundary at the ancient town of Thetford. What I looked for now were Coke's beginnings, his boyhood, every trace I could unearth of his parentage, the houses where he had grown to manhood, the school where he learned his Latin grammar. In London, Lambeth, Buckinghamshire, I had visited the scenes of Coke's old age and middle life — crowded scenes, with an air of grandeur about them, an air of the world, of great men and events . . . The House of Commons in session, the members seated in tiered rows, face to face, as they had sat when Coke was Speaker, like a church choir about to sing . . . Coke's country house at Stoke Poges where he died, with the Hatton arms above the fireplace, the tall gates in the park adorned with Coke's crest.

In Norfolk I sought a different air, a different ethos altogether — and long before the advent of those calamitous monarchs, King James and King Charles I. Modern times began, it has been said, in the latter years of Queen Elizabeth. But now I went behind modern times — back to feudality almost, back to the bad old days of Mary Tudor, who came to her throne the year that Coke was born — the unhappiest young queen, I think, who ever wore a crown. The Norfolk of Coke's boyhood retained much of medieval outlook toward the land. There were still bondsmen and bondswomen on the manors, the lord held court in his great hall, dispensing justice. Three-quarters of Britain, moreover, was still Roman Catholic; the English Reformation was only just gathering strength, with its blood and terror, its martyred heroes and shattered stone saints, its real and written influence upon the common law.

Coke's youth and early manhood saw a revolution in attitude not only toward religion but toward the land and its ownership. The *Strangers* came, as they were called, pouring into Norfolk across a narrow channel to the port of Yarmouth — men of Antwerp and Amsterdam, Walloons and Dutch who knew how to dyke the Norfolk fens and how to weave the wool that was to make Norfolk rich and raise Norwich to be the second city of England, "as large within the walls as London," Coke boasted. Sheep devoured the common lands and starved the peasants. When hedges were cut down and sheep grazed in pastures that had been plowed land, Norfolk saw fighting rebellions, men hanged in chains from the walls of old Norwich Castle. . . . Two hundred years passed, and the sheep that had been the poor man's curse became his blessing. Coke's own eighteenth-century descendant won celebrity for his experiments in sheep breeding. *Coke of Norfolk,* this descendant was called; I had heard much about him since I came to England.

As actual itinerary for my trip, I listed Sir Edward's Norfolk houses and his farms, the school he had attended as a boy in Norwich, his books and library at Holkham House on the North Sea and his tomb in Tittleshall Church, near the village of Mileham where he was born. I wanted to see the ancient castle of Blancheflower, rising on its high mound, and the shire house nearby, where in the year 1607, when Coke was made a judge, he said farewell to his old friends, the citizens of Norwich. "For he that is a judge, ceaseth to be a friend; in judgment no acquaintance, no remembrance of forepassed, present or future hope of friendship must direct the thought." There was an old portrait of Sir Edward in Norwich Guildhall, I had been told, done when he was a young man. And according to the records, Coke's Norwich house still stood, down by the river Wensum, half of it medieval, built by the Pastons, and half Elizabethan, added on by Coke. I wanted to see the beautiful country house called Blickling, built by Coke's friend and colleague on the bench, Sir Henry Hobart, and I wanted to walk along the ocean cliffs near Cromer, where Coke and his father had owned property.

In this seeking, I hoped to find more than the records promised — some shard, some shell that would give off an echo of things not written in the books. During my weeks in England, I had evolved a view of the past, illusory perhaps, but useful. I had come to look on history as a circle, made up of two great arcs. The lower arc was the past, the upper arc the present that grows upon the past. Only when the two arcs touched, could one hope to experience history, make brief and vital contact with what went before.

It was a fanciful conception, but to me as real as work, as real as Monday. Before crossing the Norfolk border I had found, after desperate hunting and many false turnings in my car, Coke's old manor of Huntingfield, where he had lived in his early manhood and where many of his children were born. In Coke's day the house had been enchanting. The great hall was built around living oaks which supported the roof as they grew; on the branches, archers hung their crossbows as they hurried in to dinner. When I came there, nothing was left of the original mansion. In its place I saw an ugly raw brick villa, inhabited by a young couple who rented the three hundred acres and farmed them.

Yet when, beyond the machine-made furniture and modern kitchen, I came out upon Coke's green terrace, I saw the cattle standing on the marshy fen below, as Coke's cattle surely stood on such a hazy August afternoon, four centuries ago. Across the little stream I saw the arched bridge that I had read of. "Come with me up the hill," the farmer said. "I want to show you something." He was a retired Air Force pilot, in his early forties; he had a flourishing red mustache, the hardest blue eye and the pleasantest laugh of my experience. It seems that when he planted his oats, one spring, they came up in a geometric circle. Ten centuries earlier, the field had been the site of an Anglo-Saxon encampment. In a grape basket, the farmer showed me his collected shards and pieces; the museum people at Norwich had assured him they were true Saxon relics. "Two bowshots from the house," I told him, in my turn, "there is an old oak tree. Queen Elizabeth came here to visit, and she sat in the oak and shot at deer with her crossbow."

The farmer nodded briefly and led me across four fields. The oak at its base was huge, its trunk split by storms and age, its great branches shattered. Quite obviously, it could not have been less than four centuries old. The farmer fetched his saw and cut me off a board — a substantial piece of wood, too long to fit in my car. When I drove off, the board stuck out the back, beyond the door. (In New York when the customs man saw it, he said he didn't know about Queen Elizabeth, but if I cared *that* much, I could take it home.)

The present and the past, today and yesterday. If the relics that I clung to were ridiculous, it is to be remembered that I sought, on this Norfolk pilgrimage, no crumbling temples revered for their beauty, no portraits for their "art," but everything for its likeness to what had been, its powers of evocation. I found Coke's Grammar School in the Cathedral Close at

Norwich, under the shadow of the great spire that dominates the city. A hundred years before Coke's time, the school had been the chapel of a monastery, where monks sang masses for the souls of the dead. Now in mid-twentieth century it was still in daily use, the schoolmaster told me, though in this holiday time the room was empty of scholars. Standing in the doorway with the bleak sun seeping down through arched narrow windows, I saw that it would need no future powers of imaginative reconstruction to describe this vaulted chamber. I had only to take my pencil, now, and write the dimensions as they were.

But I wondered if Coke had been often beaten by his masters. The tales of English schoolboys, scarred by floggings, were awful; I had read of eardrums broken, and of a boy sent home from Eton chained between two greyhounds. An English friend of mine, an old Harrovian, had told me cheerfully enough of his beatings at school, adding that the one which did him most good had been wholly undeserved, given for an offense he never committed. Life, this man added briskly, delivers many an undeserved beating before we are through; perhaps it is well to learn, early, that the world is cruel and that most of its punishments are "undeserved." Stripes heal, even when the wound is wicked, and flesh grows round the scars.

It is hard to know, sometimes, if a man becomes a scholar because of his education or in spite of it. That Lord Coke was a true scholar, not even his enemies denied. Yet during the six years of his grammar schooling and three years at Cambridge University, the educational world had been altogether preoccupied with noisy religious feuds, with battles between High Church and Low. Coke and his friends had seen the stone saints smashed in the Cathedral. They had been told that Latin was the language of a gentleman and they must learn it, and then had been forbidden to say their prayers in Latin because it smacked of Rome and popery. Norfolk and Cambridgeshire were the centers of unrelenting Protestantism. In a ditch beyond Norwich walls the martyrs had been burned when Mary was Queen of England; the Bishop of Norwich was himself a returned Marian exile. When Mary died and a Protestant Elizabeth succeeded her, Norwich set about taking its revenge.

Yet how seductive, this beauty of high Cathedral arch and limitless, shadowed nave. ("I wonder," John Adams had written in his diary, "how Luther ever broke the spell.") In no cathedral of England did I feel the conflict of the Reformation so strongly as in Norwich — perhaps because I spent so many hours in the church and so much time walking alone in the Cathedral Close. Lord Coke had been no Puritan, but a Church of England man. To him, religious persecution was wicked only when it was Roman Catholic — or "Spanish"; the words became synonymous. "Toleration" to Coke was a term for weaklings and turncoats, not for rulers and judges who must establish the power of the state against foreign enemies, against armadas by sea and infiltration by Jesuit missionaries on land. If I could stay in Norwich for a year, I thought, if I could see this hilly city by day and by evening, in fog and sunshine, summer and winter, and hear the bells ring each Sunday from this score of churches — then surely I could understand Coke's early education. I would know it through sound and sight and slow absorption of the past.

Yet Coke had been no city boy; in the long holiday he

had ridden home to Burghwood, his father's estate at Mileham parish, some twenty-five miles west of Norwich and a like distance south from the marshes of Holkham and the North Sea. I said good-by to Norwich and drove westward. In the fields the harvest was nearly in, the stubble showed yellow, the high haystacks were covered for winter. Cloud shadows raced across the heath, in the afternoon the wind turned bitter cold. Coke's father, a barrister, had been a gentleman farmer; I knew some of the problems that had beset him in this meager sandy country. Coke's England grew no clover, no carrots, cabbage, turnips — no winter feed for its cattle. By spring the little short-horned cows had dwindled very lean indeed. "Twixt Christmas and May, weak cattle decay," said old Tusser in his handbook. Coke's father had surely read Tusser, and Coke read it, too; it was the sixteenth-century farmer's Bible. But meat was hard to come by, in those days. In a glass cage at Norwich Museum I had seen a family of birds bigger than turkeys. Bustards, they were called; they had roamed the countryside, fair game and good eating. Moreover, there had been no nonsense about shooting game on the wing. If game stood, there was meat for dinner; if it sat on its eggs there was meat for supper, too.

In London I had glimpsed the luxuries of Elizabethan living — at Hampton Court, at Greenwich Palace and in Coke's own beautiful estate at Stoke. Houses with a score of chimneys, with fifty rooms. I had seen inventories of tapestries and velvet hangings worth a ransom. Here in Norfolk, things were plainer. Coke's boyhood must have inured him to physical discipline, to hard work and a hard climate. Yet in Coke's youth the older generation was forever warning their young against ease of living and the new Italianate softness that was sifting into England from below the Alps. "We see the change," one chronicler had written, "for when our houses were builded of willow, then had we oken men; but now that our houses are come to be made of oke, our men are not onlie become willow, but a great manie, through Persian delicacie crept in among us, altogether of straw, which is a sore alteration."

When I came to Tittleshall it had begun to rain, a driving mist that penetrated one's bones. I got out of my car at Tittleshall church and made my way inside, reflecting that a little Persian warmth and delicacy would be welcome. For the biographer there is melancholy, something truly dispiriting, in visiting the tomb of one's subject. I found Coke's sepulcher in the chancel, a large, elaborate affair, at the corners of which knelt four female figures, draped after the classical manner. I stood and stared, my spirits sinking every minute. Here I was, trying my best to resuscitate the young Edward Coke a schoolboy on his father's farm, and there he lay before me in effigy on a marble tomb, bearded, wearing the judge's skullcap. All around moreover were the tombs not only of Coke's forebears but of his descendants in succeeding centuries, those Cokes who had been created Earls of Leicester, builders of the palace known as Holkham House. . . .

Coke of Norfolk — why, his tomb was bigger than Sir Edward's! I was tired indeed of this Coke of Norfolk, with his Holkham palace and his cattle breeding; he seemed almost to dwarf the great Sir Edward. Whenever, in London or Norwich, I had chanced to tell a well-born Englishman that I was writing about Coke, he had replied at once, "Oh, of course, Coke of Norfolk! Fine feller, did wonders for sheep breeding. Friend of Turnip Townsend, wasn't he? Great admirer of your George Washington. Have you been to Holkham House, on the North Sea?"

Yet it had been Sir Edward, not Coke of Norfolk, who had founded this family and its fortune. Every one of the present Earl of Leicester's forty thousand Norfolk acres had been acquired, so I was told, by Sir Edward Coke. . . . I turned and fled the church, got in my car, slammed the door against the rain and drove on to look for Godwick, Coke's small country house, or what might be left of it. *Tittleshall-cum-Godwick,* the village was written on the map. At Brown's Hotel in London, my gray-haired, dignified chambermaid, Lily Balders, came from "Tittashawl," as she pronounced it. She had told me so many local tales that I knew the village intimately, together with its inhabitants, not excluding a certain disagreeable family with whom the Balders were feuding.

The road was narrow. On each side spread barley fields; cows stood beneath the trees. The cows were wet, and so was what was left of the barley; the trees dripped water, the sky was a sodden gray. But somehow I felt better, with every quarter-mile my spirits rose. . . . When I got home, would the things I had found outweigh the things I had not found? Coke's seven sisters, for instance. Here in Norfolk the boy grew up with seven sisters, no less. Winifred, Ursula, Dorothea, Ethelreda — they bore romantic Saxon names. I cherished a fancy psychiatric picture of how their existence had molded Coke's character, what they did to him and he to them. Yet I had not, so far in Norfolk, discovered one thing about the seven sisters beyond the identity of their husbands. My readers were going to have to remain in the dark concerning all these significant siblings — who came first or last, whether the girls were older or younger than their brother. I thought of the

Old Parliamentary History that I had studied at home — two dozen volumes, written by heaven knows how many candid contemporary pens. "We have now a Gap of Time," wrote one of these historians, "of near four Years, and nothing material to fill it up with."

Plainly, there were to be Gaps of Time in my account of Coke's boyhood. Yet the prospect did not depress me. There was so much to tell! It was an embarrassment of riches rather than a dearth. Here in England the past rose up so strong it frightened me; it is hard for an American to feel permanently easy in a country that does not know the word *frontier*. In Norfolk the names were as English, the people as homogeneous as they had been in Coke's day. I had come to know these surnames: Gawdys, Townsends, Clippesbys, Hobarts — cousins that intermarried pleasantly. No farmer, born Waleski, planted his beans in Norfolk as in Connecticut he plants them today in land that once belonged to an Adams or a Winthrop. England makes no ceremony of welcome when a foreigner becomes a citizen. Indeed, I had been irritated more than once when English people repeated my name after me. "Bowen? But you don't seem at all like an American. And why should an American want to write about Sir Edward Coke?"

I was American, and American I would remain. With luck, my book itself would tell why an American was a logical person to write about Chief Justice Coke. As for Sir Edward, he was an Englishman indeed, but he was also a Norfolkman, first and last. That much I had learned for sure, in these country days. . . . Not far from Tittleshall church, I found what was left of Coke's house at Godwick — a piece of chimney, the outline of a room in brick. Coke had loved this modest house more than all the glory of the ninety-six estates he managed to acquire before he died. When he was a prisoner in the Tower of London, an old man alone in a cold cell, Coke had been very homesick and with a piece of coal for a pen he had written his misery in Latin: *"Heu! horridus ille locus* . . . Alas! this place of horror. May God return me one day to my small house at Godwick."

The farmer's wife who had led me to the ruins, left me on some urgent business of her own. I stood by myself, the Norfolk mist on my face, bells from the church a mile away fading and gathering in the wind. In London I had seen a letter from Coke to Lord Treasurer Burghley, worrying about his wheat in the rainy weather. It would rot in the fields, he wrote, "unless God of his mercy do send a more seasonable time to ripen." The letter had been dated August, 1597, when Coke was Queen Elizabeth's Attorney General, with much on his mind beyond corn and crops. But to an English country-man his land comes first — before wife and child, perhaps. And this spot, the muddy field where I stood, had been Coke's land. The merciless hard wind that broke the hedges, the rain that drowned the wheat, to Edward Coke had been the sound and feel and dear responsibility of home.

The park gates at Holkham are two miles from the house. *Palace* would be a better word; it is one of the most imposing of England's great country mansions, filled with treasures that a king might envy. Sir Edward Coke never saw either house or park; it was built by his descendant, Thomas of the name, first Earl of Leicester, a century after Coke died. Sir Edward's library was what I had come to see; nearly all of his books are housed here. Dr. Hassall, the present Earl's librarian, expected me; we had been in correspondence. The young Lord and Lady Leicester were in residence, Hassall said; I had replied that I saw no reason to trouble them with my requests or presence. Not an earl but a scholar was what I needed, to show me the books. (It is my experience that noble lords are more knowledgeable concerning horses, soldiering and game birds than they are about old books and parchment.)

It was Saturday morning when at the gates of Holkham Park I rang the porter's bell for the first time. A cross old man, white-haired, came out of his house and requested my pass; no one could enter in a car without written permission from his lordship. "But I am to meet Dr. Hassall in the Earl's library at nine-thirty," I said, adding that I had come all the way from America.

The porter made it plain that he cared little for America and less for Dr. Hassall. I might leave my car at the gates if I chose, and walk to the house. This was Saturday and Lord Leicester didn't favor trippers in cars. I reached for my purse and thought better of it; Dr. Hassall had warned me not to tip this man: "It will only make it harder for the rest of us." I turned my car round, hurried to the hotel, found a Cambridge clergyman with whom I had fallen into conversation at breakfast, borrowed a bicycle from him and pedaled back uphill to the gates, prepared this time to do real battle. At my ring the porter emerged, looked at me, looked at the bicycle, grunted, and unlocked the big ironwork gates.

It was exhilarating, whizzing along the long, curving driveway in the crisp morning, between the great trees and lawns and fields. I had not ridden a bicycle in years, but it held me upright. The house when I came to it was enormous, the

color of yellowed sandstone, severe in the eighteenth-century
classic manner, with wide wings and a paved terrace behind
tiers of steps. Before the circular driveway a herd of deer
cropped peacefully, lifting their heads as I went by. Everywhere, sheep grazed. From a little lake by the house, ducks
rose with a clatter of wings.

Dr. Hassall was wating at a side door. "You are late," he
said, and without inviting explanation, led me inside, saying
that we would go up to the library by the back way, it was
quicker. As often as I visited that enchanting place, I never
was able to find my way upstairs alone. Dr. Hassall walked
fast, with a bouncing, eager gait. He was a man of about my
own height, in his forties. Dark straight brown hair fell over
his forehead, his eyes were large behind a scholar's spectacles.
In winter he served as librarian in Duke Humfrey's Library
at Oxford. Already, this summer, he had taken me over the
Bodleian, with its incredible treasures and its celebrated wall
sign: "Tread lightly, speak little."

Now I trotted after Hassall up an infinity of corridors,
banked and stored with the relics and furniture of a great
house . . . old portraits of forgotten cousins, of favorite game-
keepers and bailiffs and hunting dogs. I caught a glimpse of
galleries and state chambers, all crimson brocade and gilded
chandeliers. We passed by stone statues in niches, marble-
topped tables, urns and busts, and came suddenly upon the
portrait of George Washington, with a plaque beneath it,
signed *Coke of Norfolk:*

"*Every day during the American War did I drink the
health of George Washington as the greatest man on earth.*"

The library, when we found it, was white and gold, with
pointed arches over the doors — as beautiful a room as I ever

saw in my life. It held twenty thousand volumes; Coke's own books numbered over three hundred and were housed in a small square room adjoining. Wide windows faced down across the park; above the fireplace was a portrait of Charles James Fox, looking cynical and worldly. Only a part of Coke's library was in this room, Dr. Hassall told me; the rest was upstairs in a tower, where he would take me later in the day. The best of the volumes were shelved high, he said; no use having visitors pawing at them.

It was a feast of books. Coke's own parchment catalogue formed a roll forty-two feet long, signed by him at intervals down the skins. Here were his lawbooks — a *Registrum Brevium,* said to have been given to Coke by Queen Elizabeth, and all of Sir Edward's collected works of literature, with which I hoped to confound the pundits who like to say that Coke was illiterate in all but law. Aesop's *Fables,* Boccaccio's *Decameron,* Machiavelli's *Prince,* and his *Politics, Orlando Furioso,* Plutarch's *Lives.* There were presentation copies of books on law and history, from friends of Coke's whom I had come to know as if they were my uncles: John Selden, the brilliant legal scholar, a handsome creature whom the ladies favored; William Camden, the historian, whose works I loved; Robert Cotton, the antiquarian, so enamored of old records in the Tower of London that when the keeper would not lend them, Cotton used to slip the records under his doublet, carry them home across the city and "forget" ever to return them.

A ten-foot ladder was pushed toward me. I settled it squarely on its four legs and climbed up, pencils behind my ears and notebook in my teeth. Perched on the ladder top, at once I was lost to the world. Here in Coke's handwriting were the notes for his lectures at the Inner Temple in the year 1592, on the *Statute of Uses*. Seven lectures in law French, leather-bound and written clearly. Coke's usual hand was cramped and atrocious. I remarked on it. "This is Coke's *tidy* writing," Hassall said, and inquired if I had seen, at the British Museum, the old copy of Littleton's *Tenures*, with Coke's inserted lines giving the main facts of his life. His *Vade mecum*, Coke had called it. I said yes, I had seen it but I could not have deciphered it if I had not known what it said by heart before I came to England. "Less educated men wrote better hands," Hassall reminded me. Writing was, after all, a mere clerkly art.

Here at my shoulder was a leather-bound *Collection of Pleadings*, copied beautifully, and here the *Proceedings against Lord Bacon in 1624*, in a careful clerkly script. I saw books with the armorial bindings of Sir Christopher Hatton, and perhaps three dozen volumes bearing Sir Edward's arms or his crest — the ostrich with a horseshoe in its beak.

While I paged and read and studied on my high perch, Dr. Hassall sat below me at a round, leather-covered gaming table, typing busily. He was answering queries from Los Angeles, California, he said, concerning Coke's copy of Fitzherbert's *Abridgment*. I told him I had just come across the household accounts of Coke's first wife, Bridget Paston, in the year 1596–1597. Clutching to my bosom a parchment-covered volume, I backed down the ladder and sat across the table from Dr. Hassall, copying lines and trying not to exclaim aloud with pleasure at what I found:

"Tewesday. Item. Leekes to make the poore folkes porridge. . . . Item. Eleven swyne for the provision of the house. . . . Leaf gold to gild pastry withal, whyte wyne to boyle capons withal . . ."

It was all set down in a steward's hand, overlooked and signed each week as "Discharged by me, Bridget Coke." The steward had tried out his penmanship on the blank sides of the pages, with round flourishes in the sixteenth-century manner. *"Dorothy,"* he wrote. *"Doro . . . Doro . . . the end of all my Joy and all my . . ."* The last word was illegible. Who then was this Dorothy, I wondered? Did the steward love her hopelessly, and what did Bridget Coke think when she came across these flourishes of an enamored pen? "Dorothy?" said Hassall. "Probably a bitch hound of the steward's. Dorothy is a good name for a hound. But be careful in your copying — Tutivillus may be looking over your shoulder."

Tutivillus, it developed, was a fiend, a devil, collector of liturgical and typographical slips made by monks when they copied manuscripts. *"Démon des copistes,"* Hassall said. Tutivillus first appeared in the thirteenth century, but there was no reason to think he had been exorcised, now in the year of our Lord 1951. . . . Next after Bridget's account book I saw a tiny, bound copy of Magna Carta, with Coke's notations thick along the margins. Sir Edward had adored Magna Carta and was forever quoting it in Parliament, or to his law students. "And it is called Magna Charta," he said, "not in respect of the voluminousness of it but of its importance."

There are unkind critics who hint that Coke read into Magna Carta things that were not there; Coke "invented" Magna Carta, they say. And in truth, Sir Edward resurrected the old parchment copies at a time when England badly needed a charter of freedom, something ancient and authoritative to refer to when Stuart kings forgot the people's rights. From the famous Chapter 39, Coke translated *legem terrae* as "the common law . . . No freeman shall be imprisoned *nisi per legem terrae*" — unless, Coke said, "by due process of the common law, the native, English law."

Dr. Hassall and I traversed more corridors, that afternoon, and climbed winding stone steps in a tower. At the top we found a quiet room, lined with books, sunny and delicious. A window faced south. Half a mile down the park I saw the tall obelisk, built by the first Earl, among the trees. In the lake, cows stood to their bellies; ducks sailed toward the terrace.

Up here, Sir Edward's books were shelved with the fore edge outward, in the sixteenth-century manner. On the lip of the bindings I could see old marks for chains to tie the volumes to the shelf, against marauders. I sat on an overturned box and began to read; I hoped that Dr. Hassall would not hurry me from this room. It was the first time I had been warm in Norfolk . . . I saw the Year Books in black letter, bound together, eight or nine at a time, again with Coke's marginal notes. (How I like a man who cares enough about his books to write in them, and what a boon it is to biographers!) There were books of history and theology in their original vellum bindings, and the manuscripts and lawbooks out of which Coke had garnered his own immense knowledge and had compiled his *Institutes*. Here were the *Works* (*Opera*) of Bellarmine, that mighty Catholic apologist. I thought of King James I and his long arguments with Bellarmine, all carefully composed by the hand of majesty and sent abroad. Surely, this James Stuart was the oddest figure of a king who ever sat on a throne, with his baggy Dutch trousers, his rolling gait and slobbering lips. A man essentially good-natured, who would have made an excellent Church of England bishop, with time off for hunting the stag between ecclesiastical duties.

Here at my hand was a book on sorcery, printed in Paris in the year 1508. Sir Edward Coke believed in witches, of course. So did Sir Thomas Browne, the Norwich physician, half a century later. Reasonable enough, for devout men; if a person did not believe in witches, how could he believe in angels and thence in God, whom the angels served? Coke's *Third Institute* has a chapter on "Felony by Conjuration, Witchcraft, Sorcery or Inchantment." Sir Edward included lines translated from the *Odyssey,* descriptive of "inchanters":

> *By rhymes they can pul down full soon,*
> *From lofty sky the wandring moon.*

I had found every word fascinating. It was felonious, Coke said, to conjure up a wicked spirit, even if one gave the spirit no command to action. Any practicing to cause a neighbor to "waste or pine" was a felony, and any taking of bodies from the grave to use skin or bone for witchcraft or enchantment. There never was a lawbook that made such good reading as Coke's *Third Institute;* in its pages one saw the whole long pageant of Elizabethan life.

I could stay forever in this high quiet room, I thought, with the Victorian engravings on the walls. "The Departure" . . . "The Empty Saddle." . . . Up and down Holkham Park I went each day on my borrowed bicycle; when it rained I drove my car; the Earl's butler wrote me out a pass and the gatekeeper honored it. Dr. Hassall and I had lunch and then dinner with the Earl of Leicester, his pretty blonde Countess and the nice old Nanny who had cared for their three children. To the Earl, my interest in Sir Edward Coke was incomprehensible. Why should an American, and a woman at that, want to write about Sir Edward Coke?

I did not try to explain, but conversed with his lordship about sailing small boats — something I knew from my youth — and about the care and upbringing of deer, a subject strange to me until that morning, when I had paged over a pertinent volume on the gaming table. In the long twilight of a Tuesday night I cycled out of Holkham Park for the last time, removed my clothes from the postmistress's best bedroom, where I had been housed, and next morning in my little car headed southwest, for Cambridge.

All the way down through Norfolk, the countryside was reminiscent of Lord Coke. . . . Castle Acre, with the great Norman gateway, the church and Saxon cemetery. The estate of Castle Acre had belonged to Coke, who purchased it when priory lands still were bargains. . . . Stiffkey, where Nathanial Bacon lived, brother to Sir Francis, and a House of Commons man. No one in Stiffkey village knew the name of Bacon. I would not have found the old house but for a man in a pub who called the village *Stukey,* and laughed at my pronunciation. "Oh, you want the old 'all," he said.

Stiffkey with its round high towers, its sunken gardens with their faded beautiful brick walls . . . Cambridge and the narrow High Street . . . Trinity Great Gate, where Coke as a young man had walked beneath the archway, his short black undergraduate's gown swinging with his tall frame. The University does not favor women, does not particularly favor Americans as purveyors of English history. All that day and the next, challenges came thick as hornets, thick as arrows, aimed at the eye. In Trinity College dining hall I stood with a don, looking at Sir Francis Bacon's portrait on the wall. "No man more extraordinary ever lived," I said. "At his impeachment, Coke stood beyond the bar of the House of Lords . . ."

I was talking, I think, to myself, wondering if I could do that impeachment scene full justice in my book. "I take it," the don replied morosely, "you plan to write a popular book about the Chief Justice?" It would not be possible to reproduce the despair with which he pronounced the word *popular*. "At least" (this was a second don) "you have been shrewd enough to see that a book about Lord Coke will sell." . . . "Oh well," said a third don, at tea that afternoon, in rooms overlooking Trinity Great Court. "Oh well, Mrs. Bowen possesses a certain courage, perhaps. We must remember that a person has to begin to learn *some*where."

There is a marvelous turn and trick to British arrogance; its apparent unconsciousness makes it twice as effectual. The dons, of course, knew exactly what they were doing and knew that I knew it. Consigning them at once to a hell peopled only with female scholars, I made my replies with equal blandness. Next evening in London I met a fourth don from Cambridge, professor of criminal law and a great student of legal history. I did not tell him of my experiences at Trinity College. But I talked about Lord Coke, about the English common law, about Coke's parliamentary career and the gratitude that I, as an American, felt toward this man. Smarting from the pricks of yesterday, I asked the professor at some length what he thought of my approach to the problem and to this biography of Lord Coke. My questions must have emerged with a troubled note, for the professor turned and laid his hand on mine. He is Polish, and his accent rolls like a C string on the cello. "Write about Lord Coke? But of course!" he cried. "This will be your gr-reat adventure!"

On the last night but one of my visit to England, an evening of full moon, I went by taxi down to Tower Hill, got out and walked alone above the walls and the dry moat. It was an eerie, awesome sight, the white keep in the center, the clouds moving above, and southward the river, broad, majestic and secret under the moon. I returned to the gates at ten o'clock, just as the guard was changing. Out came the Warder in his scarlet watchcoat, keys in hand. An order was barked and answered from far off, in the shrill singsong of the British command.

Three hundred and fifty years ago, Lord Coke had heard that sound at night from his Tower cell, an old man and a prisoner. . . . How could I leave this country, where every stone was reminiscent? How could I go home and write about Lord Coke in a world as new, as different from this one as Birmingham is different from Baghdad?

Standing by the Tower moat I thought of old John Hacket, writing his biography of a certain Bishop Williams; I had learned by heart what he said in his preface: "How shall I defend that I am constant to mine own Judgment in this Design, and that I thrust my Labours into the World? What Warrant can I plead, that I build a new Cottage upon the Waste?"

What warrant indeed, and why should an American want to write about Lord Coke? How many times had I been asked the question, here in England? I got into my taxi, the driver slammed the door as we rolled over the cobbles and I finished the quotation to myself:

"Measuring my Strength," the old historian had said, *"by my own Meet-wand, I task my self to set up a Pillar but for one Man's Memory."*

Index